Superstars

OF STOCK CAR RACING

Superstars

OF STOCK CAR RACING

FRANK MORIARTY

MetroBooks

MetroBooks

An Imprint of Friedman/Fairfax Publishers

©1999 by Michael Friedman Publishing Group, Inc.

Library of Congress Cataloging-in-Publication Data

Moriarty, Frank.
    Superstars of stock car racing / Frank Moriarty.
        p.   cm.
    Includes bibliographical references (p.) and index.
    ISBN 1-56799-881-X
    1. Automobile racing drivers—United States Biography. 2. Stock
car racing—United States—History.   I. Title.
GV1032.A1M67 1999
796.72'092'273—dc21
[B]   99-32608
                                                                       CIP

Editor: Nathaniel Marunas
Art Director: Kevin Ullrich
Designer: Lynne Yeamans
Photography Editor: Valerie E. Kennedy
Production Director: Karen Matsu Greenberg

Color separations by Radstock Reproductions Ltd.
Printed in England by Butler & Tanner Limited

10 9 8 7 6 5 4 3 2 1

For bulk purchases and special sales, please contact:
Friedman/Fairfax Publishers
Attention: Sales Department
15 West 26th Street
New York, NY 10010
212/685-6610 FAX 212/685-1307

Visit our website:
http://www.metrobooks.com

Dedication

Rather than being dedicated to a single person, this book is dedicated to an entire group of people—namely, the drivers of yesteryear, whose on-track exploits in the era of primitive safety measures and little or no sponsorship made the phenomenal success of today's racers—not to mention the Winston Cup Series as a whole—possible. This volume is a tribute to the courage, dedication, and skill of these rough-and-tumble men.

Introduction

The nations of the world are always associated with the sports that in some way contribute to their cultural identity. In Great Britain, sports like cricket and soccer color the grand picture of British life. Canadians have never been shy about their love of hockey. Italy and France have turned out more than their share of daring downhill skiers.

In the United States, first baseball and then football helped define the young nation's persona. But, in the boom years immediately following World War II, the United States became known for something else. It was a feature of society that symbolized an economy on the go supported by citizens on the move—the car. Is it any wonder that a sport has grown up around the national fascination with the automobile? And is it at all surprising that this sport has experienced astonishing growth in the relatively brief fifty years of its existence?

Sure, Americans were always interested in motorsports, as the proud history of the Indianapolis 500—dating back to the beginning of the 1900s—makes clear. But those cars were exotic vehicles, built exclusively for racing. Stock cars were a whole other matter, and racing them proved to have overwhelming popular appeal to the American driver at large.

When Big Bill France began to build the National Association for Stock Car Automobile Racing, just after the end of hostilities in Japan and Europe, he envisioned fans flocking to NASCAR tracks to see races between cars that looked just like the cars cruising the streets of the United States. Today we marvel at his prescience.

Of course, it was far from France's only profitable insight into the nation's psyche—in fact, the man was a marketing genius (and his son Bill Jr. has proven himself no less shrewd in recent years). The elder France's clairvoyance about what race fans would want to see is the foundation upon which today's Winston Cup Series is built.

Not that the fifty-year ride has been all smooth. NASCAR has had to stand firm in the face of controversies ranging from disastrous accidents to automobile manufacturer pullouts. In more recent years, a host of new problems have arisen, ranging from keeping the cars racing at relatively safe speeds (below 200 mph [320kph]) to the manufacturers presenting models that require significant profile massaging to fit within NASCAR's rules. Even the tradition of two-door coupes has yielded to the acceptance of four-door sedans. At the end of the day, naturally, the troubles of administering stock car racing are always more than compensated for by the excitement that unfolds on the track.

Despite all the obstacles along the way, the rich history of NASCAR continues to gain additional color with each passing season. This book is a celebration of that rich history and especially the heroic men behind the wheel who have brought that history to life in season after season of asphalt-blistering stock car racing action. As they say before every race: "Drivers, start your engines!"

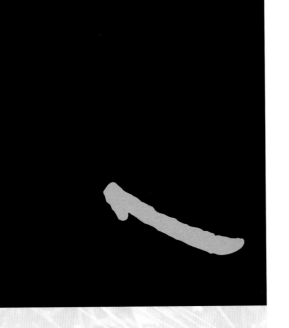

Dirt, Sand, and Moonshine

The roar begins to swell. It is the sound of an excited crowd of hundreds of thousands of people. As they rise to their feet, all eyes focus on the same spot. Row after row after row of fans are aligned in towering grandstands that stand sentry on the outer perimeter of a miles-long tri-oval of pavement. The paved ribbon itself surrounds hundreds of vehicles and thousands more spectators. As one, the assembled masses look to the fourth turn of the tri-oval where the pavement tilts, banking at a severe angle.

There, slowly navigating through the turn, are forty brightly-colored vehicles, adorned with a chaotic patchwork of logos and identification numbers. These are the cars of the NASCAR Winston Cup Series. Inside the cockpits of these incredible machines sit the superstars of stock car racing.

As millions of viewers at home lean towards their television screens, the pack of cars begins to pick up speed. Each grinding touch on the accelerator brings a proportional increase in volume. The mechanical chorus deepens, expands, grows louder still, drowning out the sounds of the race fans. As the cars near the starting line, a green flag waves from the flagstand. And...

NASCAR's greatest drivers are now unleashed, the stock cars streaking into competition mere inches apart as their speeds rocket toward the 200 mph (320kph) mark. This is the excitement that has made stock car racing the hottest sport in the United States in the 1990s.

At the turn of the millennium, NASCAR and its flagship Winston Cup Series are big business. Want to sponsor a top Winston Cup team? You'll need roughly $8 million, give or take a million or two. But it's all worth it—more than six million fans will see your car race each season, and millions more will watch on television.

And it all began in a smoke-filled hotel conference room in Daytona Beach, Florida, in 1947.

If anyone in that room could have imagined where stock car racing was going to go in the future, it was Bill France, Sr., or "Big Bill." France was a man of vision who believed in stock car racing, was sure that he could guide the sport to national prominence, and ruled with a iron hand. That there are now superstars in stock car racing is a direct result of the foundation France built beginning at the Streamline Hotel on December 14, 1947.

OPPOSITE: **Chaos reigns on the old Daytona course in 1953, as several drivers find their chances for victory dashed in a multicar pileup.**

France had summoned every influential stock car racing personality he could think of to the meeting at the Streamline. There were car builders, drivers, and promoters—all part of what was a more-or-less disorganized sport. France aimed to change all that.

When the series of meetings had ended three days later, France and the thirty-five participants had created an organization called the National Association for Stock Car Auto Racing—NASCAR. Over the years, it would come to represent the pinnacle of U.S. motorsports.

But not in the beginning—that distinction had to be earned, a process that began as the new sanctioning body conducted races through the late 1940s and into the 1950s. It began in the South, with drivers whose training included stints running moonshine on darkened roads in the depths of the night. Men brave enough to outrun federal agents in vehicles frequently overloaded with liquid contraband didn't find the prospect of racing each other on a speedway that

intimidating at all. And in the process, they put on one heck of a show.

As word spread about NASCAR competition, more and more fans were drawn to the race tracks. France began to sanction events outside the South, spreading his organization's influence and helping bring order to U.S. motorsports.

On June 19, 1949, in Charlotte, North Carolina, a new NASCAR division competed for the first time. It was called Strictly Stock. France's idea was to have the cars competing look like the cars the fans were driving; this would help them identify with the stock car drivers. The Strictly Stock division would evolve into the Grand National Series, and then eventually be re-christened the Winston Cup Series.

But in NASCAR's first decade, the Winston Cup Series was a long way off. Racers often drove to the tracks in the same cars they proceeded to drive in actual competition. But despite such humble beginnings, one element common to every NASCAR race since was

in evidence from the very first stock car race onward—the competitive fire of the men behind the wheel. These great drivers were the first superstars of stock car racing.

Buck **Baker**

At the wheel of a 1948 Kaiser, Buck Baker took the flag to start the June 19, 1949, race in Charlotte, North Carolina. Competing in the Strictly Stock division, Baker would quite likely have been amazed had he known that this race would one day lead to today's modern Winston Cup Series. Buck finished that legendary race in eleventh place. Though it was a respectable finish, Baker would go on to finish NASCAR races much higher in the standings many times in his great career.

In 1952, Baker won for the first time in NASCAR's top stock car division, taking his Hudson Hornet to victory in competition in Columbia, South Carolina. The next season, Baker won

BELOW: **In the days before drivers began roaming the garage area with public relations staff in tow, NASCAR's finest were easily accessible. Here Buck Baker (left) and Tiny Lund (right) talk racing at Daytona in 1971.**

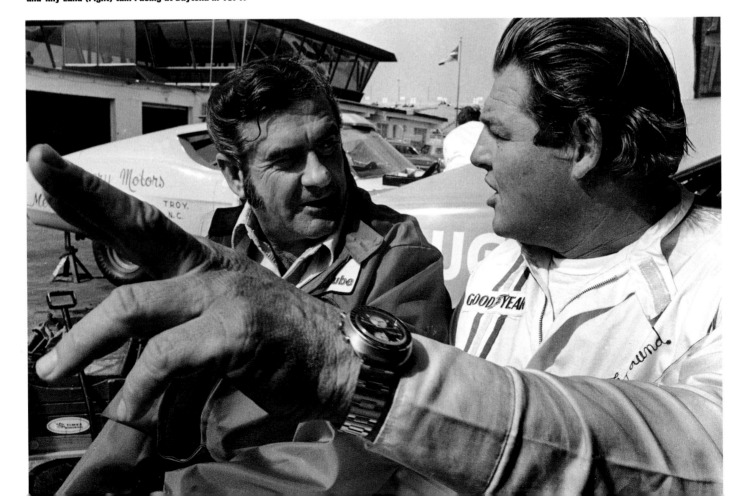

the Southern 500 in Darlington, South Carolina, a race that was NASCAR's season highlight. At the time, Darlington was NASCAR's first and only super-speedway; Baker would win the Southern 500 again in 1960 and 1964.

By the time he retired from competition, making his final NASCAR start in 1976, Baker could look back on a career that included forty-six victories and the NASCAR championships of 1956 and 1957. Baker went on to found the highly regarded Buck Baker Racing School, a motorsports educational program with a list of graduates that includes modern Winston Cup Series star Jeff Gordon.

Flock **Brothers**

In the first decade of NASCAR racing, one of the most imposing presences in on-track competition was the team of Bob, Fonty, and Tim Flock. The three brothers combined to win sixty-three races between NASCAR's inception and 1961, when Tim became the last of the three to retire from racing.

The oldest of the brothers, Bob, attended the now-legendary meeting at the Streamline Hotel in Daytona in late 1947. As such he was witness to the birth of nationally organized stock car racing. In 1949 he traveled to Hillsboro, North Carolina, where he won the third NASCAR Strictly Stock race ever held. Finishing the season third in points, Bob won a total of four races in his thirty-five career starts.

Middle brother Fonty was also a strong competitor—and a fan favorite as well. Although known as a practical joker, Fonty approached his driving seriously and was responsible for nineteen victories in just 154 races. His background as a Modified racing champion helped him when he arrived on the Grand National scene. One of Fonty's biggest victories was the 1952 Southern 500 at Darlington Raceway. In typical lighthearted fashion, Fonty emerged from his car wearing shorts and singing the traditional song "Dixie."

ABOVE: **Tim Flock cut a dashing figure, and was popular with early NASCAR fans. Though Flock had a wild sense of humor, his career racing statistics are formidable.**

Despite the success of Bob and Fonty, it was youngest brother Tim who had the most enviable record of the Flock brothers. In 187 races, Tim went to victory lane thirty-nine times—an amazing winning average of 21 percent, a record that stands to this day. Tim was a two-time Grand National champion, claiming the title in 1952 and 1955.

Tim was also known for his humor, and, in one of the most bizarre footnotes to NASCAR history, actually had a rhesus monkey named Jocko Flocko ride with him for several races in 1953. At that time drivers had a small hatch in the stock car floors which they could open to check tire wear. Jocko got loose in Tim's car, opened the hatch and was struck by a small piece of debris. The monkey went berserk, forcing Tim to

surrender the lead and remove the enraged monkey from his car. Tim Flock still managed to finish third despite his simian sidekick's antics. Jocko Flocko retired from competition following that incident.

Paul **Goldsmith**

Paul Goldsmith began competing in the Grand National Series in 1956, and his strong runs indicated that he was a bright new talent who could help guide NASCAR's top series into the 1960s.

Among the most colorful characters in NASCAR history is car builder Smokey Yunick. Yunick hired Goldsmith to drive for him in 1957, building the team's Fords out of Yunick's

Paul Goldsmith (left) and Earl Balmer (right) were the winners of the 1965 qualifying races for the Daytona 500. Their happiness stems from having secured excellent starting positions in NASCAR's biggest race.

famed Daytona Beach racing operation known as "The Best Damn Garage in Town." A tireless innovator, Yunick had cars win eight times in Grand National competition, with four of those victories coming in the 1957 season with Goldsmith at the wheel.

The final race held on the combination road/beach course at Daytona Beach took place in February 1958. This was where NASCAR and Big Bill France had promoted their first races. Goldsmith won the historic event, which symbolized the evolution of the sport of stock car racing.

Paul Goldsmith went on to compete in the Grand National Series into the 1960s, winning three times in 1966 while driving for the Chrysler-backed team of Nichels Engineering.

Junior **Johnson**

When Junior Johnson won five races in 1955, his third season in Grand National racing, it was clear the former bootlegger was poised to make an impact on the sport of stock car racing. But Johnson's legacy goes beyond his record as a driver. He became an influential car owner and helped change the face of NASCAR.

Johnson maintained that his aggressive skills as a race car driver had been developed by outrunning federal agents—"revenuers"—in cat-and-mouse chases through the hills of North Carolina, hauling moonshine. Regardless, Johnson won fifty NASCAR Grand National races, averaging one win for every six starts. In 1960, one of his finest years, Junior won both the Daytona 500 and the World 600. Johnson's abilities and reputation attracted writer Tom Wolfe, who documented Johnson in a profile for *Esquire* titled "The Last American Hero."

Johnson retired as a racer in 1966, but fielded cars for other drivers for nearly three decades. His record as a car owner was every bit as remarkable as his driving record: Johnson-owned cars won an impressive 140 victories in 838

starts. Among those wins were two Daytona 500s, three Firecracker 400s, eight wins at Charlotte, ten at Darlington, and five at Talladega.

Johnson also played a role in bringing series sponsor R.J. Reynolds and its Winston brand to NASCAR. Approached by Winston in 1969 about sponsoring his race team, Junior suggested that the manufacturer instead get

in touch with NASCAR about joining up with the series itself rather than just one team.

When Johnson retired his team after the 1995 season, he clearly voiced his concerns about the direction the sport was taking. Junior felt that the new money coming into the sport created a hostile environment for the people who had founded the sport and invested

BELOW: **A smiling Junior Johnson in 1964. His competitors rarely saw the pleasant side of Johnson during a race. Many rate him as NASCAR's all-time toughest competitor.**

their lives in it. Since Junior Johnson left NASCAR racing, the teams of NASCAR legends like Bobby Allison, Bud Moore, and Cale Yarborough have been forced out of business.

Jim **Paschal**

Jim Paschal was there at the beginning. On June 19, 1949, Paschal competed in NASCAR's first Strictly Stock race, held in Charlotte, North Carolina. It was not only the beginning of stock car racing's meteoric rise, but of Paschal's long and successful career behind the wheel.

Though Paschal only managed a twenty-third place finish in that historic race, he competed in NASCAR Grand National events for more than two decades and helped build the foundation for the sport's success today. Paschal competed in 422 races and won twenty-five of them.

LEFT: The spoils of victory are bestowed upon Jim Paschal after a hard-fought win in 1970. Paschal has just won a 250-mile (400km) event. BELOW: One of NASCAR's classic duels, as the legendary finish of the 1959 Daytona 500 unfolds. Johnny Beauchamp in car 73 battles side-by-side with Lee Petty in 42, both men determined to win the inaugural running of the February classic. OPPOSITE: A Hemi engine's view of the Petty Enterprises braintrust, seen in 1964. Mechanical genius Maurice Petty is on the left, founder of Petty Enterprises and father Lee Petty is in the center, and son Richard—NASCAR's "King"—pays attention on the right.

In the 1950s and 1960s, many of the Grand National races were contested on dirt tracks or small paved ovals, with race lengths well under 100 miles (160km). But at Charlotte Motor Speedway, the inception of the World 600 was intended as a test of both speed and endurance. The 600-mile (960km) race was longer by far than any other event on the schedule; Jim Paschal managed to win NASCAR's longest event twice, both times driving a Plymouth.

Lee **Petty**

The legendary status of the Petty name among fans of stock car racing was just being established when Lee Petty ran his first NASCAR race, which was also NASCAR's very first Strictly Stock race.

Although Lee Petty crashed in the landmark event, he would go on to found a family racing dynasty that grew along with the sport.

From a humble shop operation in rural Level Cross, North Carolina, Petty began building his family's legacy. In the 1950 season, Lee finished second in the series championship. He would have won the title if Bill France, Sr., seeking to enforce loyalty to his growing sanctioning body, had not penalized Petty by deducting points for Lee's participation in a non-NASCAR race.

But the NASCAR title did not elude Lee Petty for long, as he won the first of his three championships in 1954 and then went on to claim back-to-back titles in 1958 and 1959. Before retiring in 1964, Petty visited victory lane fifty-four times in 427 starts.

The year 1959, when Petty won his third NASCAR championship, was an important one as NASCAR struggled for respectability. That season marked the opening of Daytona International Speedway, and Lee Petty played a pivotal role in the running of the very first Daytona 500, a race that has

become legendary. The event ended in a photo finish, with driver Johnny Beauchamp declared the winner over Petty. But so close was the finish that a photo review was conducted. Three days after his car crossed the finish line, Lee Petty was awarded the title of winner of the first Daytona 500.

Marshall **Teague**

Marshall Teague was one of the first NASCAR drivers to build a reputation as a constant threat to win during the first races of the sanctioning body's stock car competition. Sadly, though, Teague's promising career was cut short.

Before the construction of Daytona International Speedway, racing in the coastal Florida city was conducted on a unique course that was part paved road and part beach. In 1951, the season opened with Marshall Teague competing in his Hudson, a brand that at the time was one of the most competitive in NASCAR. Teague captured that first event of the season, averaging more than 80 mph (128kph) in the process, despite the inherent difficulty of racing on two radically different surfaces. Teague won four additional times in 1951, helping cement his reputation as one of NASCAR's stars.

In February 1959, though, Teague was driving in a test session at Daytona International Speedway, the new superspeedway that made the old beach-road course in Daytona obsolete. At the wheel of the experimental Sumar Special, Teague had turned a lap of 174 mph (278kph). Pushing the car to its limits, Marshall Teague lost control and was killed in the resulting crash.

Herb **Thomas**

Herb Thomas was yet another racer who was a participant in NASCAR's first Strictly Stock race in June 1949. And though Thomas only managed a twenty-ninth place finish in that legendary race, during his decade-long

stock car career Thomas established himself as one of the young sport's most talented drivers.

Thomas competed in NASCAR as the sport began its incredible growth.

OPPOSITE: **Herb Thomas (left) and Smokey Yunick (right) have just won the 1954 Southern 500 in Darlington. Yunick's preparation of the team's Chevrolet gave them an edge, but Thomas' driving skill was as big a part of the winning formula at the challenging track.** ABOVE: **NASCAR was always known as a southern sport, but stock car star Marshall Teague (left) went a step further and took his Hudson Hornet South of the Border to race with co-driver Les Snow (right) when the duo went road racing in Mexico.**

In 1951 and 1953, he was the series champion. He drove in Plymouths, Oldsmobiles, and in Hudsons owned by Marshall Teague. Thomas also drove Fords in the beach racing days for Smokey Yunick, the legendary proprietor of Daytona Beach's "Best Damn Garage in Town." Yunick's mechanical abilities and innovations teamed with Thomas' considerable driving talent created a potent racing operation.

Over the course of an oustanding NASCAR career that ended in 1962, Herb Thomas won a total of forty-eight races.

Speedy **Thompson**

Multicar racing operations are considered a necessity in modern Winston Cup racing, but the concept was first successfully implemented in the 1950s by Karl Kiekhaefer. Kiekhaefer's Chrysler team traveled in specially con-

LEFT: **Before the huge superspeedway at Daytona was built, racing was held on the Daytona beach/road course. Curtis Turner makes the transition from pavement to sand behind the wheel of a Ford in 1956.** ABOVE: **Crossing the fingers can't hurt when it comes to planning for victory in the Daytona 500. Richard Petty (left) and Curtis Turner (right) hope for the best in 1967. Turner had the advantage of starting on the pole, but the race was won by Mario Andretti.**

Kiekhaefer that Thompson's career was elevated to a new level. In 1956, Thompson won eight races, setting up a streak of four years in a row in which he finished in the top three positions of the championship battle.

In 1956, Thompson narrowly lost the most prestigious race of the season, the Southern 500 at Darlington International Raceway, his Kiekhaefer Chrysler almost catching Curtis Turner. In 1957, Speedy Thompson refused to be denied NASCAR's biggest race, winning the Southern 500 at the wheel of a Chevrolet.

Curtis **Turner**

Curtis Turner was heartened by his performance in the first Strictly Stock race. Unlike many of his fellow drivers who would go on to compete in the Grand National Series, Turner managed a respectable finish (ninth place) in that historic first race.

Turner's first win in NASCAR's stock car division came just three races later in that same first season, and from there Curtis built a reputation as one of NASCAR's stars. Indeed, in 1950 Turner won four times, and swept to three more victories the next season.

In nearly two decades of NASCAR racing, Turner built a winning record and captured many of the most prestigious races on the Grand National schedule. Chief among these was victory in the 1956 Southern 500. From the first running of the Southern 500 in 1950, this South Carolina race was NASCAR's most important until the first Daytona 500 was run in 1959. Curtis Turner won the 1956 race in his Ford by holding off Speedy Thompson, who was driving one of the powerful Chryslers.

When Curtis Turner died in a private plane crash in 1970, he was remembered as one of the early luminaries who had helped put stock car racing on the map.

structed car haulers, and the professional appearance of the team was matched by its performance on the racetrack. One of the Kiekhaefer team's most important resources was driver Speedy Thompson.

Thompson first competed in NASCAR in 1950, and won his first races in 1953. But it was with

He-men and Heroes

In the early days of the Grand National Series, stock car racing drivers had reputations as hard drivin', hard fightin', hard drinkin' men who were as tough as the little bullring tracks that made up the majority of the stops on the NASCAR schedule. Though the Grand National division was NASCAR's elite level of competition, that competition was most definitely down-to-earth.

Not that the fans of stock car racing's formative days were necessarily model citizens, either. Stock car racing had a reputation for grandstands that were as wild as the action on the track. Women were frequently discouraged from attending races, and if they did there was a fair chance they'd find sufficient boozing and brawling to match the stories.

In fact, on one memorable occasion, the fans literally took over a stock car race. It happened on August 13, 1961. Deteriorating track conditions at Weaverville, North Carolina's short track led to a suspension of racing activities. An angry mob of four thousand held the competitors hostage until darkness fell and the situation was defused.

It was obvious that if NASCAR was to fulfill Bill France's vision of stock car racing as a national sport, things had to change. And, at the dawn of the 1960s, there were indications that changes were underway.

In 1950, the first of the stock car superspeedways, Darlington International Raceway, was constructed. The track hosted the biggest NASCAR race of each season in the 1950s, the annual Labor Day Southern 500. But in 1959, France put the next piece of his big-time dreams into place with the opening of Daytona International Speedway.

Overcoming funding difficulties and construction delays, Bill France had his Florida speed palace ready for the first Daytona 500, held in February 1959. The new two-and-one-half mile (4km) racetrack was a full mile (1.6km) longer than Darlington's speedway, and it's safe to say the drivers of the Grand National Series arriving at the track for the first time were filled with awe. Awe, because nobody had ever imagined racing stock cars at such a huge facility and because right from the first practice sessions NASCAR's drivers were running at speeds considerably higher than those attained elsewhere.

OPPOSITE: **Modern-day Winston Cup fans may not recognize the tri-oval at Daytona International Speedway in 1963. The towering grandstands and suites that now loom over the start/finish line were at that point many years in the future.**

ABOVE: **Mario Andretti was truly in his element here at Indianapolis Motor Speedway in 1971—but Mario didn't mind heading south to mix it up with NASCAR's finest. It was a challenge the legendary driver enjoyed.**

Mario **Andretti**

In the 1960s, NASCAR was firmly entrenched in the South. But "Big Bill" France knew that it was important to continue to expand his sport's fan base. As a result, the presence of drivers like Mario Andretti, a highly recognizable name thanks to his exploits in open-wheel racing, was a welcome one in NASCAR.

In 1967, Andretti decided to compete in the Daytona 500. He aligned with Ford and was given a car prepared by the legendary Holman-Moody team. Starting in twelfth position after qualifying, Andretti charged into the lead in

Imagine going from a one-third-mile (.5km) dirt track with flat turns to a seemingly endless, paved surface with turns banked at 31 degrees.

On February 22, 1959, the first Daytona 500 led to a photo-finish and an indication of the kind of competition to come in the decade about to begin. Lee Petty and Johnny Beauchamp crossed the finish line side by side, wrapping up 200 laps of competition, with Beauchamp being declared winner of the race. Sixty-one hours later, a review of all available film yielded a new winner: Petty. The thrilling finish and the controversy over who had actually won helped focus attention on NASCAR's organized stock car racing.

With the proven success of speedway racing at Daytona and Darlington,

the 1960s became a decade of raceway construction. NASCAR's Grand National Series sped through the decade at an assortment of new tracks, including Charlotte Motor Speedway, Michigan International Speedway, and Alabama International Motor Speedway, today known as Talladega Superspeedway.

The new tracks became ideal showplaces for the talents of NASCAR's top drivers, as the move away from dirt tracks and tiny short tracks led to thrilling side-by-side duels on high-banked turns. The battles waged in the 1960s have become some of NASCAR's most legendary, and the men who competed in that time are recalled now as some of the greatest superstars of stock car racing.

under 25 laps. He ran up front most of the race, leading for most of the laps but also burning precious fuel. A late race caution flag saved Mario's day, allowing him to conserve gas on the final laps as the race ended under caution. It was a one-two sweep for Holman-Moody, as the only other car on the lead lap was Fred Lorenzen, another of the team's drivers. Mario's win in the 1967 Daytona 500 was his only NASCAR victory.

Although Mario Andretti never fully dedicated himself to a career in stock car racing, starting just fourteen races, he was welcomed by the regulars of the Grand National circuit who enjoyed testing their skills against such a well-known driver.

Darel **Dieringer**

One of the top talents in the Grand National series, Darel Dieringer was a contemporary of many legends of NASCAR including Richard Petty, Cale Yarborough, David Pearson, and Fireball Roberts.

The majority of Dieringer's starts came between 1963 and 1967. Darel's first two wins came twenty-seven races apart in 1964, driving a Mercury for famed team owner Bud Moore.

Although the Daytona 500 was the most highly publicized event on the Grand National schedule, victory in the Southern 500 was always held in highest regard by the drivers themselves. The egg-shaped Darlington track is extremely

BELOW: **The narrow track at Darlington is blocked completely in 1964 by Junior Johnson in the 27 and Darel Dieringer in the 16. H.B. Bailey makes contact with Dieringer, but Ned Jarrett in the 11 snakes by the wreck.**

difficult to race on, as the turns are a different radius at each end of the speedway. Drivers hit the wall so often attempting to get through the turns that the damage sustained by the cars is known as a "Darlington stripe." But in 1966, Dieringer conquered the track that's often described as being "too tough to tame," and won the prestigious Southern 500.

In his Grand National career, Darel Dieringer won seven races in 181 starts.

A.J. **Foyt**

In the 1970s, the International Race of Champions was founded. The idea was simple—take superstars from different types of motorsports, and have them compete in equally prepared cars in a series of race to see who is best.

But before there was an IROC series, it was not uncommon for open-wheel racers to be bitten by the stock

car bug. Like Mario Andretti, A.J. Foyt was tempted to see what he could do with a heavy stock car hurtling around a superspeedway, and the drivers of the Grand National Series were happy to race against such a famous competitor.

Of course, NASCAR's resident competitors may not have been so happy about Foyt's presence had they been queried after the 1972 Daytona 500. The Texan, provided a Mercury by the famous Wood Brothers race team, proceeded to dominate NASCAR's highest profile event, crossing the finish line to win the race over Charlie Glotzbach, who trailed Foyt by nearly two full laps. It was the second time in six years that a driver better known for performances in the Indianapolis 500 had won the Daytona 500, following Mario Andretti's Daytona win in 1967.

A.J. Foyt never competed in more than seven NASCAR events in any one season, but in just 128 total starts he went to victory lane seven times.

BELOW: **The man who won in nearly every series he competed in, the great A.J. Foyt, climbs from his Chevy at Daytona International Speedway after winning the pole for the 1976 Firecracker 400. Foyt was also fastest qualifier earlier in the year at the Daytona 500.**

Ned **Jarrett**

The early days of stock car racing are often recalled as a period of time when drivers were likely to be battling a hangover as well as a stock car's handling, when arguments were settled with fists, and the garage area was like the wild west of the frontier days. That was the environment when one of stock car racing's true gentlemen, Ned Jarrett, began his racing career in 1953.

So bad was the reputation of racing that Jarrett's first efforts in competition came under an assumed name. But as his confidence on the racetrack grew, Jarrett began to compete under his own name, starting his first Grand National races in 1953. Though he did become known as "Gentleman Ned," Jarrett knew that racing against men like Junior Johnson and Curtis Turner required the occasional show of force, and when challenged he would not back down. But his intelligent approach to NASCAR racing led to great success.

Although he won the 1961 championship, Jarrett's best years came at the wheel of cars fielded by car owner Bondy Long. Ned claimed fifteen wins in 1964 and thirteen in 1965. His Grand National series championship in 1965 was the first for Ford Motor Company.

Jarrett left an impressive career record behind when he retired in 1966 at the young age of thirty-four. But his influence on NASCAR would continue. Ned Jarrett took a Dale Carnegie course in an effort to improve himself, and eventually moved into the field of broadcasting. Since then he has become one of racing's most respected motorsports commentators.

Fred **Lorenzen**

In the NASCAR of the 1960s, Ford's Holman-Moody team was held in high regard, much as Hendrick Motorsports and Roush Racing are in the 1990s. And one of the greatest drivers to compete for the legendary team was Fred Lorenzen.

Lorenzen had first begun to compete in organized stock car racing near his home in Illinois, eventually racing in United States Auto Club competition. But the lure of NASCAR drew the young driver to the South, where he found employment in Holman-Moody's shops. Still, Lorenzen wanted to race, so he left his job and attempted to break into the Grand National Series. By the end of the 1960 season, after only a handful of starts, Fred was in dire financial straits. He was forced to sell all of his racing equipment at a loss, and return to his native Illinois.

Then, late in 1960, came a phone call that changed Lorenzen's life. It was from Ralph Moody, asking Lorenzen to return to the Holman-Moody operation—as a driver. Lorenzen made the most of his big break, winning three times in the 1961 season. By 1962 he had climbed to seventh in the championship points standings, and in 1963 became the first Grand National driver to surpass the $100,000 mark in season earnings. As

TOP: **Ned Jarrett has reason to smile in 1965, having just won the Southern 500 at Darlington, a true "driver's race." Miss 500, Vicki Johnson, looks on in approval.** BOTTOM: **Fred Lorenzen in 1960, when NASCAR stock cars really were nearly stock vehicles off the street. As Lorenzen's career progressed over the years, the cars became more and more specialized as competition vehicles.**

his Holman-Moody team only competed in select Grand National events, it's quite likely that Lorenzen could have won the championship instead of finishing third in the standings—if only his team had raced in all of the events.

Lorenzen shocked the racing world when he retired in 1967, a decision he still regrets. Fred returned to NASCAR racing in 1970, but hung up his helmet for good in 1972, winner of twenty-six races in a relatively brief career.

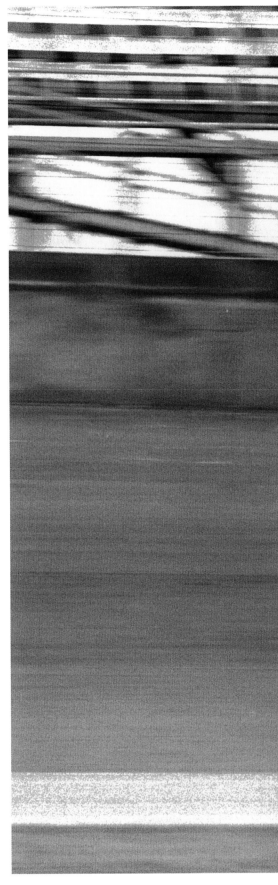

ABOVE: **Tiny Lund was anything but tiny, his stature dominating the driver's seat at Daytona in 1970. Lund was a fan favorite during an era many consider to be NASCAR's most competitive.** RIGHT: **Testing in the weeks leading up to the Daytona 500 is a necessity. Here Tiny Lund guides his Dodge Charger Daytona past empty grandstands in early February 1970.**

Tiny **Lund**

Dewayne Lund was a racer, and a big man. So of course, his fellow competitors thought the perfect nickname for the six-foot-four-inch(192cm), 270-pound (122 kg) driver was "Tiny."

After racing motorcycles, trying his hand at dirt track racing, and even racing Sprint cars, Lund got off to a tremendous start in his Grand National career. Could there be a better first victory than a win in NASCAR's most important race, the Daytona 500? That's exactly how Lund kicked off his career in 1963.

It was a race that Tiny Lund wasn't even supposed to be in. The Wood Brothers car that Lund steered to victory lane was scheduled to be driven in the Daytona 500 by Marvin Panch. But Panch was involved in a terrific crash at Daytona while testing a Maserati sports car. The car caught fire as a result of the crash, and Tiny was one of the first people on the scene aiding the injured driver. Too hurt to compete in the 500, Panch asked the Wood Brothers to give

Lund a chance. The rest is history. Lund held off Fred Lorenzen in the Holman-Moody Ford to win the February classic.

Lund went on to win four more races in NASCAR's top series and was also a two-time champion in the Grand American series. Attempting to return to racing in the Winston Cup Series after a two-year absence, Tiny Lund was killed on August 17, 1975, after crashing at NASCAR's fastest track, Talladega Superspeedway in Alabama.

Richard **Petty**

For a driver with such a remarkable career—one that includes NASCAR starts in five decades—it is difficult to decide which period best represents Richard Petty's amazing legacy. But it was in the 1960s that Petty truly ascended to superstardom, bringing the sport of stock car racing into greater national prominence.

The son of NASCAR racing pioneer Lee Petty, Richard was a young twenty-one-year-old who had racing

fever when he asked his father for a try-out behind the wheel in July 1958. Richard took an Oldsmobile convertible to a race in Columbia, South Carolina, and returned to the Petty home base in Level Cross, North Carolina, with a sixth-place finish.

Named NASCAR's Rookie of the Year in 1959, Richard soon found himself competing against his father. The younger Petty discovered that family relations meant nothing in stock car racing; what looked to be Richard's first win, at Atlanta in 1959, was taken

away when Lee demanded a scoring recheck. The results of the tally caused the win to be taken from the son and given to the father.

But Richard's career path seemed set, and his first Grand National win came at Charlotte early in 1960. Petty

never looked back. In 1964, Petty won his first Daytona 500 and was declared series champion at the end of the season, the first of his record seven titles.

In 1967, Richard won an astonishing twenty-seven races on his way to his second series championship. By the time

winner, with fifty-five of his wins coming on NASCAR's fastest tracks, and he also holds the record for most consecutive Winston Cup wins with ten-in-a-row during the 1967 season.

Known as "The King," Petty's behavior out of the race car was anything but haughty and regal. His work to popularize stock car racing can not be underestimated. Petty's fame may have come from winning, but his popularity with race fans can be attributed to his willingness to spend hours signing autographs and meeting the people who bought tickets to watch him race. Petty set the standards for driver conduct by which all modern Winston Cup competitors are judged.

After retirement, Richard Petty continued to campaign his familiar number 43 car as a car owner, with several drivers trying to fill the King's imposing shoes. The team struggled in modern competition, but Bobby Hamilton finally returned Richard Petty to victory lane in 1996 and 1997.

he retired from competition in 1992, Petty had tallied many figures that were equally remarkable. His career winning average is an extraordinary 17 percent, generated by winning 200 times in 1,177 starts. Aside from being NASCAR's all-time race winner, Petty is also the all-time pole winner with 126 starts from the fastest qualifying position. He is the all-time superspeedway race

ABOVE: **Sometimes delicate tweaking of aerodynamics gives way to plain old brute force. Strategically positioned in the trunk of his car, Richard Petty fixes some damage with a good hard kick at Atlanta in 1979.** BELOW: **This time it's Richard Petty waving after winning here at Michigan in 1975, but the man in the car next to Petty, David Pearson, certainly won his share of the legendary showdowns that took place between these two men, both of them among NASCAR's greatest.**

Fireball **Roberts**

Edward Glenn Roberts became one of NASCAR's first superstars as the sport desperately sought to establish itself. It truly needed a marquee name, and "Fireball" Roberts fit the bill.

First competing in the Grand National Series in 1950, Roberts set a blazing pace in his career. His first win came in only his third start, at Hillsboro, North Carolina, on August 13, 1950. It was the first of thirty-three wins for the legendary Fireball Roberts.

Truth be told, Roberts colorful nickname had been bestowed upon him long before he entered NASCAR racing. He was called Fireball because of his pitching arm, but the imagery certainly carried over into his later career. But as flamboyant as Roberts' runs were on the track, the man himself could best be described as a reluctant superstar. Rather than parade around, Roberts focused on his race cars.

In 1958, he won the Southern 500 at Darlington Raceway. The fan favorite became even more popular as the 1960s dawned. In 1962, he won the Daytona 500, and the next year repeated his Darlington feat.

By 1964, Fireball Roberts was considered the biggest star in stock car racing. So it came as a tremendous blow to the sport when Roberts was grievously injured in a terrible crash at Charlotte Motor Speedway on May 24, 1964. Running early in the World 600, Roberts was unable to avoid getting caught up in the crash of Ned Jarrett and Junior Johnson on the backstretch. His Holman-Moody Ford backed into the wall and burst into flames. Jarrett made a heroic effort to rescue his friend, but Roberts was badly burned. Since he suffered from asthma that was aggravated by the early flame retardants used on the clothing of the day, Roberts' untreated driving suit had provided little protection and his burns were very severe. Weeks later, on July 2, the beloved Fireball Roberts succumbed to complications from his burns and died.

ABOVE: **A common sight in NASCAR racing through the 1960s was Fireball Roberts holding the winner's trophy. Here Roberts is seen at the 1962 Firecracker 400.**

ABOVE: **As NASCAR progressed through the 1960s, even Miss America took notice. Mary Ann Mobley reads the inscription of Joe Weatherly's trophy after he won a Daytona 500 qualifying race. Fireball Roberts, behind Mobley, won the other qualifying race.** OPPOSITE: **Joe Weatherly's fatal crash at Riverside, California. The disastrous accident on January 19, 1964, marked the loss of one of NASCAR's first superstars.**

Joe **Weatherly**

In an era of increasing competition in NASCAR's Grand National Series, Joe Weatherly managed back-to-back championships in 1962 and 1963.

Weatherly came to NASCAR an experienced motorcycle racing champion, having collected three American Motorcyclist Association championships in the late 1940s. And though he took his racing seriously, Weatherly also brought with him a well-deserved reputation as a practical joker—the kind of personality common in what were quite likely NASCAR's most colorful years.

Weatherly claimed his first win in 1958, but in 1961 and 1962, his win total each season was an impressive nine victories. In 1962, Weatherly won his first Grand National championship, repeating the feat in 1963 although only winning three races.

As the 1964 NASCAR Grand National season dawned, Weatherly looked ready to go for his third straight championship when tragedy struck. On the 86th lap of the January 19 race at the Riverside, California, road course, while racing in car owner Bud Moore's Mercury, Weatherly hit the wall in what seemed merely a glancing blow. Not wearing a shoulder harness, though, Weatherly had not been restrained properly in the car and his helmet had made contact with the wall. When track rescue crews got to his car, they discovered that Joe Weatherly had died from the impact.

Writing the Record Book

The tumultuous decade of the 1960s had been a good one for NASCAR and organized stock car racing. The sport saw a boom in the construction of new superspeedways, and the cream of NASCAR's drivers entered into the realm of sports stardom.

But NASCAR racing had also been the battlefield in a war between the major automobile manufacturers Ford Motor Company and Chrysler Corporation. The old racing expression "Win on Sunday, sell on Monday" had been taken to heart by both companies. The result was a fleet of racing teams benefiting from full corporate backing. Petty Enterprises was the elite Plymouth team, Nichels Engineering carried the Dodge banner, Holman-Moody was Ford's flagship, and the Wood Brothers were aligned with Mercury.

The manufacturers did far more than just supply parts and financial support. As the on-track competition grew to a fever pitch, the battle moved to the desks of engineering departments and wind tunnel aerodynamicists. Ford developed the sleek Torino Talladega and Mercury Cyclone. Chrysler went them one better, dreaming up the Dodge Charger Daytona for 1969 and the Plymouth SuperBird for 1970, wild eighteen-foot-long cars with pointed snouts and huge aerodynamic wings towering over their trunk areas.

Bill France watched the battle with deep concern. There was a founding principle that France thought was crucial to NASCAR's survival—that the race fan in the grandstands be able to identify with the cars he saw racing on the speedway. France knew most fans had no interest in driving exotic cars with wings, and he took steps to reel in the increasingly bizarre aspects of NASCAR racing. He first put in place requirements that manufacturers had to build a large number of cars available to the public for any model being raced in NASCAR. When that didn't deter Plymouth from building nearly two thousand SuperBirds—the manufacturer willingly taking the financial risk in exchange for winning the Daytona 500—France placed highly restrictive engine limits on the exotic cars.

That move effectively ended "the aero wars." But there was an unexpected side effect. The manufacturers, feeling they had proved their points and gained sufficient marketing benefits in the 1960s, drastically scaled back their NASCAR racing efforts after the 1970 season. It left the teams scurrying to

OPPOSITE: **Bobby Isaac poses with the famous K&K Insurance Dodge in 1972, happy after qualifying at Daytona with a lap clocked at more than 186 mph (298kph).**

ABOVE: **The incident that changed NASCAR forever: in front of the first live flag-to-flag Daytona 500 television audience, in 1979, Bobby Allison grabs Cale Yarborough's foot in a post-race melee. The fight, coming after a heated on-track battle, helped get the nation's sports fans talking about NASCAR.** RIGHT: **Bobby Allison in the 24 Ford swerves to avoid colliding into driver Clyde Prickett's vehicle, marooned in the bank at turn four. Seconds later, Allison would also be stuck in the bank. Only eighteen of the forty-four cars entered in the event managed to finish, a statistic that would be very unusual today.**

keep their racing operations in business, and it left France justifiably concerned about maintaining the level of competition the growing fan base had come to expect. And then came Winston.

Junior Johnson had been approached by R.J. Reynolds' Winston cigarette brand as a potential sponsor for his race team. Johnson suggested the company consider sponsoring NASCAR's top series, and Ralph Seagraves, in R.J. Reynolds' sports marketing operation, saw the potential of the partnership.

In 1971, the NASCAR Grand National Series was christened the NASCAR Winston Cup Series. The season prize fund was $100,000, to be shared among the top twenty drivers.

Throughout the 1970s, much of the groundwork was laid to create a sport that has seen that purse grow toward the $5 million mark by the late 1990s. Once the series was renamed, the schedule was shortened to roughly thirty races in the season. By reducing the number of races, the idea was to get all of the teams competing in all of the races, as some of the top teams only entered events that they considered prestigious. And along with the shortened schedule came greater interest from the television networks, as well as new tracks like Dover Downs International Speedway and Pocono International Raceway.

As more and more of the U.S. audience found stock car racing broadcast on their weekend sports programs, they began to get a clearer idea of the thrills of the sport and identify with the new generation of superstars of stock car racing.

Bobby **Allison**

Ironically, the roots of NASCAR's famed "Alabama Gang" stretch to Florida, where, in 1955, Bobby Allison first began racing. The eighteen-year-old had to get a permission slip from his mother to compete in a race at Hialeah Speedway, but from those humble origins Allison would soon build one of NASCAR's most legendary careers.

After becoming involved in competition in NASCAR's Modified division, Bobby and his brother Donnie moved to Alabama, where they felt the short track racing there would be more competitive and give them a better chance at making a decent living racing.

Between 1961 and 1965, Bobby broke into the Grand National Series, then went at the circuit full-time in 1966. He reached the top ten in the season's points standings and won his first three races in NASCAR's top division. In 1971, with the Grand National division renamed the Winston Cup Series, Bobby scored eleven wins, and added ten more the very next season.

Through the 1970s and into the 1980s, Bobby was known as a fierce competitor, battling his chief rivals, Richard Petty and Darrell Waltrip. After Waltrip had won the 1981 and 1982 Winston Cup championships, it was up to Bobby to stop him. Armed with the resources of the DiGard racing team and with top crew chief Gary Nelson—the man who would one day become NASCAR's Winston Cup Series director—Allison captured the championship in 1983.

Surely one of the highlights in Allison's racing career was winning the 1988 Daytona 500. Bobby crossed the finish line just ahead of the race's runner-up—his son, Davey. It was a popular victory among fans, not surprising since the fans voted the elder Allison NASCAR's Most Popular Driver six times in his career.

The career of Bobby Allison came to an end after a wicked crash at Pocono International Raceway in 1988 left him with a severe head injury. Allison's recovery took years, and he never returned to a Winston Cup cockpit.

Donnie **Allison**

The brother of fellow NASCAR competitor Bobby, Donnie Allison was a state diving champion growing up in Florida. Although he had followed his brother's first racing efforts, Donnie had no real interest in driving himself until a friend with a car convinced him to take the wheel in a 1959 race. A racing career was born.

When Donnie followed Bobby to the fertile racing territory of Alabama, fate once again intervened. A driver on a competing team quit, and Donnie was offered the position. Donnie proceeded to hone his racing skills in the Modified class in which his brother had found success, and he scored more than thirty wins from 1961 to 1963.

In 1966, Donnie made his first start in the Grand National Series. His first win came the next season, while driving for car builder Banjo Matthews, and Donnie won again in 1968. His strong runs landed him a ride with the fabled Wood Brothers team as the 1970s

ABOVE: **In 1973 at Talladega, Donnie Allison aligns the Alabama Gang tradition with one of NASCAR's legendary racing teams, the Wood Brothers of Virginia.**

dawned and NASCAR's top series changed its name to Winston Cup.

But Donnie's success was not limited to NASCAR racing. A.J. Foyt called, and Allison went to the Indianapolis 500. Driving for the demanding Texan, Donnie scored top-ten finishes in the 1970 and 1971 races at historic Indianapolis Motor Speedway.

With ten wins in NASCAR's top division in just over 240 starts, Donnie Allison helped cement the legend of the Alabama Gang.

Buddy **Baker**

As the 1960s dawned, Buck Baker was one of Grand National racing's most respected competitors. But a talented new driver was beginning his own career—Buck's son, Buddy Baker.

Although Buddy Baker showed flashes of his talent when his equipment was up to the task, it wasn't until 1967 at Charlotte Motor Speedway that Baker won for the first time in Grand National competition. Once he learned how to win, Baker applied that knowledge throughout the following decade. He won twice at Talladega Superspeedway, he captured the Southern 500 at Darlington, and he won three World 600 races at Charlotte Motor Speedway. Then, in 1980, Baker won the race dreamed of by every Winston Cup Series competitor—the Daytona 500.

In racing, records are made to be broken. But the only kind of record that can't be broken is when a driver becomes the first to reach a historic landmark, as Buddy Baker did in March 1970. Under the guise of testing new

---

LEFT: Buddy Baker's imposing stature in the garage area was matched by his performances on the track, featuring aggressive moves behind the wheel and a "win or else" philosophy. BELOW: The Winston Cup cars of the 1970s were much bigger than today's stock cars, and created a much larger wake through the air on superspeedways. Here Richard Petty drafts behind Buddy Baker in 1973.

ABOVE: **Pete Hamilton in Daytona's victory lane after winning a qualifying race on February 14, 1971. Hamilton was the Daytona 500's defending champion, having won the race in 1970 while driving for Petty Enterprises.** RIGHT: **Two Winston Cup champions racing side-by-side in 1973, with Bobby Isaac running high in the number 15 while Darrell Waltrip clings to the inside groove.**

equipment, Chrysler Corporation's Larry Rathgeb had asked Baker to drive a Dodge Charger Daytona at Talladega Superspeedway. The Daytona's sleek nose and wing at the rear provided unheard of stability at high speeds, and allowed Buddy Baker to become the very first stock car driver to complete a lap at more than 200 mph (320km).

Pete **Hamilton**

The Daytona 500 is always an unpredictable race, one that has on several occasions been won by someone seeking their first Winston Cup victory. Pete Hamilton is one of those first-time winners.

The Massachusetts-born driver had been slowly building a reputation in NASCAR circles through the 1960s, and when Plymouth asked Petty Enterprises to field a two-car team in 1970, Richard Petty selected Hamilton to be his team-

mate. The two men would be driving the new Plymouth SuperBird, a car with a pointed snout and a huge stabilizing wing at the rear. The SuperBird was built as a companion car to the Dodge Charger Daytona, designed by Chrysler's aerodynamicists for the racing program administered by Larry Rathgeb.

Hamilton had never driven a SuperBird until the futuristic vehicles were unloaded at Daytona International Speedway. But Hamilton—known for his aggressive charges—took to the winged car immediately. And when the Daytona 500 field took the green flag, Hamilton charged toward the front. Richard Petty's SuperBird suffered an engine failure, so it was up to Hamilton to bring home the trophy for Petty Enterprises. In a classic battle against David Pearson in the Holman-Moody Ford, Hamilton held off the experienced competitor and won NASCAR's biggest race.

Hamilton was master of the superspeedways in 1970, sweeping both races at Talladega Superspeedway. After cutbacks in Chrysler's racing program forced him out of his ride at Petty Enterprises, Pete Hamilton won his final race in NASCAR's top series in a qualifying event for the 1971 Daytona 500 while driving for car owner Cotton Owens.

Bobby **Isaac**

Bobby Isaac became NASCAR's first champion of the 1970s, a decade that was characterized by expanding popularity and media coverage. But Isaac himself was a quiet, retiring man who was more interested in his car's performance than generating fame.

Raised in near-poverty conditions in rural North Carolina, Isaac saw stock car racing as his route to success. After breaking in at short tracks, Isaac tried his hand at the Grand National Series in 1962, wining his first event in 1964 in a 125-mile (200km) qualifying race for the Daytona 500. Isaac was driving a Chrysler-backed stock car for Nichels Engineering, and it was during his

partnership with Chrysler operations that his greatest success would come.

In 1970, Chrysler had pushed the envelope of stock car racing technology with the new Dodge Charger Daytonas and Plymouth SuperBirds, exotic cars with huge stabilizing wings at the rear. While drivers like Pete Hamilton drove all-out to win at the superspeedways, Isaac's driving strategy—to take care of

his equipment and be in a position to win at the end of the race—served him well. Isaac won eleven of the foty-seven races in the season and was crowned series champion.

Isaac's championship year came when he was teamed with one of NASCAR's most brilliant and legendary crew chiefs, Harry Hyde. After the 1970 season, the two men took their team's Daytona to the famed Bonneville (Utah) salt flats and set a string of land speed records, many of which have yet to be broken.

A true racer to the end, Bobby Isaac died after collapsing in August 1977 while racing at Hickory Speedway.

Benny **Parsons**

Hailing from the mountain country of North Carolina, Benny Parsons became one of the NASCAR Winston Cup Series' most popular drivers and has graduated to the broadcasting booth as one of motorsports' most respected commentators.

Parsons worked his way through local short track racing, making his first starts in NASCAR's top division in 1964 and in 1969. Finally, in 1970, he was ready to run the full season. Impressive in his debut year, Parson managed twelve top-five finishes and almost won one race.

LEFT: **After winning NASCAR's longest race in 1980—the 600-mile (960km) event held at Charlotte Motor Speedway—an exhausted Benny Parsons isn't too tired to hoist his trophy aloft.** BELOW: **No matter the era, NASCAR short track racing results in bent fenders and crumpled sheet metal. Benny Parsons' crew assesses damage at North Wilkesboro, North Carolina, in 1978.**

In 1971, Benny Parsons managed to claim his first Winston Cup Series win, on the short track at South Boston, Virginia, driving for car owner L.G. DeWitt. The team went on to finish eleventh in the championship standings. Parsons climbed to fifth the following season, improving his standings in spite of a winless season.

The collaboration was obviously paying off for Parsons and the DeWitt team, and their consistent improvement continued in 1973. Returning to victory lane in July in Bristol, Tennessee, Benny Parsons then built a string of strong runs and held off the formidable Cale Yarborough to win the Winston Cup Series championship.

Before retiring and trading in his steering wheel for the microphone, Benny Parson won many of Winston Cup racing's most prestigious events, including the 1975 Daytona 500 and the 1980 World 600 at Charlotte Motor Speedway.

David **Pearson**

One of only two drivers to retire with more than 100 victories—the other is Richard Petty—David Pearson earned his nickname "The Silver Fox" for his cunning ability at the wheel and his ability to keep cool under the most pressure-packed racing situations.

Pearson entered Grand National competition in 1960, sweeping the Rookie of the Year title and impressing observers with his strong finishes. His first win came the next season in NASCAR's longest race, the World 600 at Charlotte Motor Speedway. Pearson followed up his first win with 104 more before retiring in 1986, winning the Grand National championship in 1966, 1968, and 1969.

When Pearson decided to drive for the highly regarded Wood Brothers team in 1972, it began a partnership that has become one of the most storied made contact, crashing and spinning across the huge runoff area at Daytona International Speedway. Petty's car came to a stop, the motor stalled. But David Pearson had the presence of mind to keep his motor running and was able to recover from the crash, slip the Wood Brothers Mercury into gear, and creep across the finish line to win NASCAR's most prestigious race.

Cale **Yarborough**

For a race driver to win at least one race every season is a tremendous accomplishment. To win a single championship is a terribly difficult feat, let alone trying to win two. But to win three championships in a row? That amazing record belongs to just one NASCAR driver, South Carolina's Cale Yarborough.

Cale struggled to break into NASCAR's top series, like many drivers before and after him. He had become intrigued with the idea of racing after seeing the famed Darlington Raceway constructed just miles from his home. His first start came in 1957, but his racing career was far from certain. Yarborough was on the verge of giving up racing when, much like another NASCAR star, Fred Lorenzen, Cale received a phone call that changed his life. Ford's Jacques Passino, head of the company's racing program, called Yarborough to offer him a ride with the legendary Holman-Moody race team, Ford's flagship operation in stock car racing.

The offer was the foundation that Yarborough needed to begin building his legendary career. Cale made his first trip to victory lane in 1965, and, in one his greatest triumphs, won his first of five Southern 500's in 1968 at the same Darlington track that had had such a profound impact on his future plans.

Yarborough's greatest years came in eight seasons associated with a man who was already a NASCAR legend, Junior Johnson. As car owner, Johnson provided Yarborough with cars that the determined Yarborough made the most of. Cale was regarded as one of NASCAR's toughest drivers, and Johnson has described

ABOVE: **Cale Yarborough was a NASCAR fan favorite. One of the toughest of all stock car drivers, Yarborough became known to many fans for carrying an early type of in-car camera for CBS and radioing his impressions of the competition during the telecast of the Daytona 500.**

in NASCAR racing. The Wood Brothers concentrated on fielding cars at NASCAR's biggest races, skipping some of the smaller events, and during his seven years with the team, Pearson racked up forty-three victories.

Pearson's most legendary win may very well be the 1976 Daytona 500. It seemed clear that David and Richard Petty were going to battle it out for the win. And battle they did. On the last lap, exiting turn four, the two cars

ABOVE: **LeeRoy Yarbrough rumbles down a NASCAR straightaway in 1969, driving a Ford Torino Cobra at the height of the manufacturer-driven "aero wars."** BELOW: **LeeRoy Yarbrough smiles contentedly after winning in Trenton, New Jersey, in 1968. In the 1960s and 1970s, NASCAR solidified its fan base in northern states.**

his driver's style as "sneaky brave." Yarborough used that style to win the championship in 1976, 1977, and 1978.

Still regarded by Johnson as his favorite driver, Cale Yarborough retired from driving in 1988 with eighty-three wins in NASCAR's toughest series.

LeeRoy began the season winning the most important race of the year, the Daytona 500. It was a race that Chrysler's factory teams desperately wanted to win, but Johnson's crew had mounted a particularly adhesive tire on Yarbrough's Ford. LeeRoy chased down Charlie Glotzbach's Dodge Charger,

getting by him on the final lap of the race and holding on to win by mere feet. LeeRoy Yarbrough also won the World 600 at Charlotte Motor Speedway, and the Southern 500 at Darlington, capping off a NASCAR dream season and elevating his status to that of racing supserstar.

LeeRoy **Yarbrough**

When the 1970s arrived, LeeRoy Yarbrough had established himself as one of NASCAR's brightest stars. The handsome Florida driver was one of the top competitors at a time when the excitement of NASCAR racing was being discovered by a larger audience.

Yarbrough found his greatest success teamed with one of NASCAR's founding drivers. When Junior Johnson retired from competition, he founded his own race team. Johnson's team was a potent force from its inception until Johnson withdrew from NASCAR in 1995. Typical of Johnson's success in fielding NASCAR stock cars was the 1969 season of Yarbrough.

4

Fresh Legends

"Big Bill" France had led NASCAR from its inception in 1947 through a period of financial stability and growth. In 1972 he decided to step down, but the reigns of power did not travel far, as France's son, Bill Jr., assumed control of the sanctioning body. The younger France has led the sport to levels of popularity that were once unthinkable, and much of the expansion came about in the 1980s.

In 1979, CBS had, for the first time, broadcast the Daytona 500 at Daytona International Speedway live from start to finish. It proved to be a tremendous opportunity for NASCAR, and the drivers of the Winston Cup Series did not disappoint the national television audience. Race leaders Cale Yarborough and Donnie Allison crashed on the final lap, yielding first place to Richard Petty. Petty managed to hold off Darrell Waltrip to win NASCAR's biggest race, a feat that was exciting enough. But Cale Yarborough, Donnie Allison, and Donnie's brother Bobby had become involved in a scuffle in the wake of the crash. The nationally-televised brouhaha had the sports world buzzing, and many curious new fans began to follow the action.

In the wake of CBS's ground-breaking broadcast, it became clear that television would be an important NASCAR ally in the 1980s. In 1981, the ESPN cable television sports network broadcast its first Winston Cup Series race. The nascent network was in dire need of exciting programming, while NASCAR needed the coverage. It was a perfect match at a perfect time.

While the "big" races on the Winston Cup schedule, like the Daytona 500, were the domain of the television networks, ESPN began to broadcast races from tracks that had never had events televised. It created a fundamental shift in the way viewers perceived NASCAR. For the first time sports fans began to get a feel for how the entire season was unfolding, seeing tracks like North Carolina Motor Speedway and Bristol International Raceway in addition to the handful of superspeedway races that had been broadcast in earlier decades.

In 1984, President Ronald Reagan contributed to NASCAR's growing legitimacy, landing on Air Force One at the airport adjacent to Daytona International Speedway. It was during

OPPOSITE: **Geoffrey Bodine, in the 7 Ford Thunderbird, leads Bobby Labonte in the 1996 Bud at the Glen, at Watkins Glen, located in Bodine's home state of New York.**

ABOVE: **Geoffrey Bodine was happy to be racing for Ed Berrier at Daytona in 1999. Forced to sell the Winston Cup team he had bought from Alan Kulwicki's estate, Bodine faced the 1999 season without a ride until Berrier put together a Winston Cup package to complement his own Busch Series efforts.**

the running of the superspeedway's Winston Cup Series Fourth of July weekend race, and Reagan made it to the grandstands in time to watch Richard Petty win his 200th and final NASCAR race. The post-race meeting between the President and the NASCAR King on the United States' biggest holiday provided invaluable exposure to stock car racing.

Throughout the 1980s, another phenomenon emerged. As many of the founding superstars of racing were retiring, their sons were beginning their own careers. It became clear that a new crop of NASCAR talent would help ensure stability of competition for decades to come.

Most important of all, the rivalries and fierce racing that characterized the 1980s were as thrilling as those of any

period in NASCAR's history. Indeed, many long-time race fans point to this decade as a golden era of superstars of stock racing.

Geoffrey **Bodine**

Chemung, New York's Geoffery Bodine has had one of modern Winston Cup racing's best careers.

Bodine began his racing activities on local tracks, before moving on to compete in the NASCAR Modified series. The Modifieds are tremendously popular in the Northeast, and the competition among the drivers is as intense as that found in any motorsport. It was here that Bodine learned many of the skills that he would need to survive in NASCAR's top series.

After a stop in the Busch Grand National Series and occasional runs in the Winston Cup Series in 1979 and 1981, Bodine ran his first full season in 1982, winning the Rookie of the Year honors.

Bodine soon teamed up with car owner Rick Hendrick, and the partnership led to three wins in 1984. In 1986, Bodine won NASCAR's biggest race, the Daytona 500. Competing against the best drivers from a variety of racing series, Bodine added the championship of the all-star International Race of Champions series to his resume in 1987. Driving first for Junior Johnson and then Bud Moore early in the 1990s, Bodine continued to win at the wheel of Ford Thunderbirds. Then, when 1992 Winston Cup Series champion Alan Kulwicki was killed in a plane crash in

1993, Bodine purchased the team and drove to three wins as team owner in 1994. But sponsorship woes forced Bodine to give up ownership of the team in 1998 and seek a new driving position for 1999.

Although his career has taken some unexpected turns, Geoffrey Bodine is still more than capable of winning in the Winston Cup Series.

Neil **Bonnett**

One of the most popular drivers in NASCAR history, Neil Bonnett was a member of the "Alabama Gang," the informal but closely aligned regional group of racers founded by Bobby and Donnie Allison.

In fact, it was Bobby Allison who gave Bonnett his first breaks in the lat-

ter's quest to reach the upper echelon of stock car racing. Fierce competitors on the short tracks of Alabama, the two men became friends off the track. And when Bobby began moving up in the Winston Cup world, he hired Bonnett to drive his cars in regional short track competition. Bonnett thrived in Allison's equipment, traveling across the country and

BELOW: **Although Geoffrey Bodine had to give up ownership of his own team in 1998, in 1999 he was able to land a new ride. Here, Bodine blazes around the track in the 60 Power Team Chevrolet Monte Carlo during Daytona Speedweek, February 12, 1999.**

ABOVE LEFT: **The lure of racing proved too strong for Neil Bonnett. Beloved by fans as a motorsports broadcaster, Bonnett couldn't stop himself from making a comeback to Winston Cup Series competition.** ABOVE RIGHT: **Dale Earnhardt pulls on his gloves, a warrior preparing for battle at Charlotte Motor Speedway. The network of tubing provides cooling to key vehicle systems, including the most important of all: the driver.**

winning dozens of races a year as he honed his driving skills.

When the time came for Bonnett to move up to the Winston Cup Series, again the Allison family helped him with the transition. After sporadic starts in 1974 and 1976, Bonnett charged to victory lane twice in 1977.

Clearly this newest member of the Alabama Gang had the same talent as its founding racers.

Though Bonnett won eighteen times in his career, he was sidelined by numerous serious injuries incurred in a series of devastating crashes. In 1985, he suffered a broken wrist at Martinsville

Speedway and a badly broken leg in 1987 at Charlotte. The broken bones healed quickly, but injuries from a crash at Darlington in April 1990 were more troubling. Bonnett suffered from amnesia in the wake of the violent impact and did not climb into a Winston Cup car for more than three years.

Away from the driver seat, Bonnett moved into broadcasting. His good humor and easygoing personality quickly made him one of the best television analysts, able to explain to fans exactly how a driver was approaching a race situation. But the lure of racing proved too strong. Bonnett, driving for Richard Childress at Talladega in July 1993, saw his return to racing end in another violent crash as his Lumina flipped over at nearly 200 mph (320kph) and crashed into the catch fence protecting the front stretch grandstands. Incredibly, Bonnett later made his way to the CBS television broadcast booth to give his perspective on the crash to the fans.

In February 1994, Bonnett was excited about another return to racing. But in a practice session for Daytona 500 qualifying, Bonnett's car broke loose in the fourth turn and smashed into the outside wall. Neil Bonnett died from injuries sustained in the crash.

Dale **Earnhardt**

He came charging into the Winston Cup Series with a force and fury that other drivers sometimes found alarming. In fact, one of the nicknames bestowed upon Dale Earnhardt is "The Intimidator." Other names used to describe him are less complimentary. If he had arrived in the Winston Cup Series with nothing more than aggression, he would not have lasted long. But almost from the beginning, the son of early NASCAR driver Ralph Earnhardt made it obvious to everyone that he spoke the language that a stock car responds to.

Dale Earnhardt's first Winston Cup start came in 1975, but his appearances were sporadic until 1979. Then, driving for car owner Rod Osterlund, Earnhardt began writing his way into NASCAR's record books. He began with the Rookie of the Year title and his first win in the 1979 season, but he followed it up the next year by winning the Winston Cup

championship in just his second full season on the circuit.

Dale moved on to drive for car owner Bud Moore in 1982 and 1983, winning more races along the way. But the real glory days were yet to come.

They began in 1984, when Dale started driving for former competitor Richard Childress. Childress had built his operation from the ground up, struggling through lean years in the hopes of building a competitive team. With Earnhardt in the driver seat, all

the pieces of the puzzle were in place. The trophies came fast and furious, with thirty-nine race wins logged during the Winston Cup Series championship-winning campaigns of 1986, 1987, 1990, 1991, 1993, and 1994.

Over the years, Dale Earnhardt had proven his abilities on every kind of race track NASCAR's top series visited. But as the year 2000 loomed on the horizon, the seven-time champion was missing one trophy that he wanted more than any other, a trophy that almost everyone would readily admit that he truly deserved—the trophy awarded to the winner of the Daytona 500.

In twenty years of trying to win NASCAR's most prestigious race, Dale had suffered frustration with each February visit to Daytona International Speedway. He had lost the race in every way imaginable, including having a tire fail while leading the very last lap of the race in 1990.

But in 1998, the years of disappointment were forgotten. Earnhardt ran up front for much of the race, as he had done so many times before. But this time, when a late race caution flag signaled that whoever reached the finish line first would win "The Great American Race," Earnhardt refused to be denied. Driving his black Chevrolet with furious determination, Earnhardt held off charge after charge and led the field to the finish line. Finally, Dale Earnhardt had conquered the prestigious Daytona 500.

BELOW: **Despite a lessening wins total in recent years after dominating the Winston Cup Series in the 1980s, Bill Elliott is still consistently voted NASCAR's most popular driver. Elliott is seen here in 1993, when he drove Fords for Junior Johnson.**

Bill **Elliott**

With most of stock car racing's team efforts based in North Carolina, it might have been understandable if racing folk turned a skeptical eye toward a family-owned and -operated racing team from Georgia that sought to break into the Winston Cup Series in 1976. But not only did the Elliott racing team break into NASCAR's top series, they soon began smashing records once they became aligned with manufacturer Harry Melling.

ABOVE: **Terry Labonte seems pensive in this 1992 photograph; at the time his NASCAR career was at a low point. A move to the Hendrick Motorsports team was in the future, though, as was Labonte's second Winston Cup championship.**

Bill Elliott made the most of the cars he was provided with, running smart races behind the wheel of his red Thunderbirds. In 1985, he powered his way to eleven wins in the season and won an unprecedented million dollar bonus from series sponsor R.J. Reynolds for claiming victory in three of four "crown jewel" NASCAR events. His quest to win the third event—the historic Southern 500 at Darlington—brought key media attention to NASCAR racing and helped make "Million Dollar Bill" a household name.

In an era of escalating superspeedway speeds, Elliott topped them all with a lap of 212.809 mph (340kph). That effort, delivered during a qualifying run at Talladega Superspeedway in 1987, will quite likely stand for the foreseeable future, as an alarmed NASCAR soon implemented the use of an engine intake restrictor plate to reduce motor

power and keep stock cars running at speeds below 200 mph (320kph). The restriction did not slow Elliott's momentum, and he captured the 1988 Winston Cup Series championship.

In 1992, Elliott left his Dawsonville, Georgia–based team to drive for another NASCAR legend, car owner Junior Johnson. But by 1995, Elliott had returned to Dawsonville with a new team. In 1997, Elliott registered his 500th Winston Cup start.

Bill Elliott's NASCAR longevity is rivaled only by his popularity. In 1998, the soft-spoken driver was voted Most Popular Driver for the thirteenth time in his career.

Terry **Labonte**

It's been said that consistency wins championships. Proof of that can be

seen in the career of Terry Labonte, a Texan whose intelligent approach to stock car racing often places him up front at the end of a long day of racing.

Labonte began his career before he turned ten years old, racing in quarter midget cars. That was the first step in a path to the Winston Cup Series.

When Labonte did reach NASCAR's elite level, he did it in style. His very first Winston Cup race, in 1978, was at the track that many drivers feel is the most challenging, Darlington International Raceway. The egg-shaped track is known as the speedway that is "too tough to tame," but Labonte came home in fourth place. It was an astonishing finish for a Winston Cup rookie. A mere two years later, Labonte won his first Winston Cup race, again at Darlington, in the coveted Southern 500. It was just the fifthy-ninth start in Labonte's career.

In 1996 Terry Labonte broke one of Richard Petty's most enduring records. Petty had started in 513 consecutive races, but Labonte shattered the King's mark and continues to extend the record with each passing season.

The record for consecutive starts is just a footnote to Labonte's impressive career. He won the Winston Cup championship in 1984 and then in 1996, with his career undergoing a renaissance thanks to a partnership with Hendrick Motorsports, won a second championship. Labonte also claimed the championship title of the prestigious all-star International Race of Champions in 1989. Through 1998, Labonte has won twenty Winston Cup races and is a constant threat to take the victory garland in most events.

Tim **Richmond**

Of all the NASCAR drivers who rose to stardom in the 1980s, none was more flamboyant than Tim Richmond, a man who won thirteen races in NASCAR's toughest series. To fans, Richmond seemed larger than life, someone whose off-track excesses could not dull his on-track talents. Sadly, his career was all too brief.

Before teaming up with car owner Rick Hendrick and brilliant crew chief Harry Hyde, Richmond had already flashed to victory lane four times in his first five seasons of Winston Cup action. But in 1986, Richmond drove the Hendrick car to a total of seven wins, adding two more during the following season. While he was winning, he was building a reputation as a ladies' man and a wild partier.

In 1987, when Richmond began to appear ill, many thought it was too much partying again. In reality, Richmond was in the early stages of a chain of illnesses that resulted in his death two years later from complications due to AIDS.

Although Richmond missed much of the first part of the 1987 season due to his illness, he returned to driving

ABOVE: **Characteristic of his attitude away from the steering wheel, Tim Richmond strikes a carefree pose along pit road in Daytona in 1987.** OPPOSITE: **Ricky Rudd at Bristol, Tennessee, in August 1998. Rudd had had a miserable season to that point, and his "one win per season" streak was in danger of ending after fifteen years. Five weeks later, Rudd managed a courageous win at Martinsville to keep the streak alive.**

in May and managed to win two consecutive races in June, at Pocono International Raceway in Pennsylvania and on the Riverside, California, road course. Those flashes of the old brilliance were to be Richmond's last. After running August 16 at Michigan International Speedway and amid concerns voiced by his fellow competitors over Richmond's lethargic condition, Tim Richmond never returned to a Winston Cup cockpit.

Ricky **Rudd**

In Winston Cup racing, one of the hardest things to cultivate is consistency. Team fortunes ebb and flow with passing seasons, and it's not uncommon to see this season's multiple race winners be shut out in the season to come.

That fact makes Ricky Rudd's Winston Cup career all the more remarkable, for Rudd has won at least one race every season for sixteen years in a row.

Rudd was named Rookie of the Year when he entered full-time Winston Cup competition in 1977, gathering ten top-ten finishes. His first win came at the defunct Riverside, California, road course in June 1983. It set a standard for winning every season that has rewarded Rudd with the third longest such streak.

Not that it's easy keeping the streak alive. In 1994, Ricky started his own team after growing dissatisfied racing for Hendrick Motorsports. Now Rudd was faced with operating his team and gathering the millions of dollars in sponsorship money needed to succeed—and driving the car as well. In 1998, his winning streak seemed to be in acute peril. With Jeff Gordon and Mark Martin winning the lion's share of races and the remaining events snapped up by well-funded multicar teams, it seemed that the streak might end at fifteen years. But Rudd was determined. Driving at the treacherous Martinsville Speedway late in the season, Rudd heroically over-

came a malfunctioning driver cooling system on a brutally hot day. He refused to get out of the scorching car and yield to a relief driver, knowing that this race was his best chance at keeping the streak alive. Bordering on exhaustion, Ricky held off Jeff Gordon's attempts to pass him and won the race. His streak extended to sixteen and counting.

Rusty **Wallace**

Many stock car racing observers are convinced that a driver who truly understands how a racecar works from a technical standpoint has a tremendous advantage. If that's true, then Rusty Wallace may have the biggest advantage of all.

A master at understanding chassis setups and how to fine-tune a stock car, Wallace began his professional stock car racing career in the Midwest-based American Speed Association. Wallace made his first two Winston Cup Series

BELOW: **Two of the leading Ford contenders do battle in Thunderbirds at Daytona International Speedway in 1996, with Rusty Wallace edging ahead of Mark Martin.** RIGHT: **Many modern Winston Cup drivers do little more than drive their race car and fulfill sponsor obligations. Rusty Wallace, however, is intimately involved with his car's setup and preparation every step of the way.**

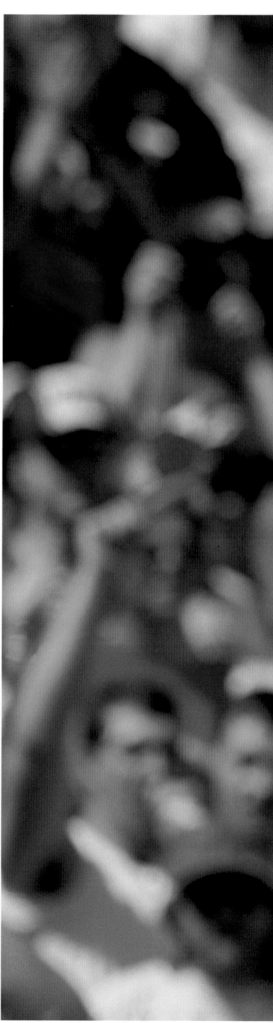

starts in 1980, even managing a runner-up finish. His first full season in Winston Cup racing came in 1984. With four top-ten finishes to his credit, Wallace was named Rookie of the Year. His first two wins came in 1986, followed by two more in 1987. Wallace upped the win tally with six victories in 1988 and 1989. The 1989 season featured a furious battle for the Winston Cup championship. Wallace escaped from the final race in Atlanta with a narrow 12-point margin to claim the Winston Cup Series championship.

In 1992, Wallace began driving for Penske Racing South, a new team owned by Roger Penske, Don Miller, and Wallace. The team won just once in its first season, but swept to victory lane ten times in 1993. This time Wallace narrowly lost the championship to Earnhardt, despite the multitude of victories.

Though his wins became fewer in the years that followed, Wallace is always a threat when running at the front of the field. A long streak without a win, beginning early in 1997, was snapped late in 1998 when Rusty won at Phoenix in the thirty-first race of the season.

Darrell **Waltrip**

In the 1970s and 1980s, Darrell Waltrip became known as much for his gift for gab as for his gifted driving performances. The outspoken driver even picked up the nickname "Jaws," managing to annoy legends like Cale Yarborough (who came up with the name) and Richard Petty off the track while beating them on the track.

After entering Winston Cup racing on a limited budget in 1972 and 1973, Waltrip won his first Winston Cup race in 1975, running at the Nashville race track where he had honed his skills in other divisions. Waltrip's talent led to his signing with DiGard Racing, and his career began to take off; he won twenty-six races with the team. As the wins piled up, Waltrip boasted, cajoled, and generally said whatever was on his mind. The racing media knew where they could go to get good quotes, and fans either loved him or hated him. But the entire time, Waltrip was helping focus attention on the sport of stock car racing.

Waltrip left DiGard to join forces with car owner Junior Johnson, himself a legendary former driver. The union flew out of the gate immediately, with Waltrip winning twelve races in 1981 and twelve more in 1982, as well as back-to-back championships to go along with the staggering win totals. In 1985, Waltrip wrapped up his third Winston Cup Series championship.

An association with car owner Rick Hendrick began in 1986. Waltrip won nine times in his first three seasons with Hendrick Motorsports' multicar operation, the most important of those wins being a victory in the 1989 Daytona 500, a race Waltrip had wanted desperately to win. In 1990, though, Waltrip experienced a winless season, in part a result of injuries suffered in a wild, end-over-end crash at Daytona's summer race.

In 1991, Waltrip formed his own team, trying to balance the pressures of car ownership and performance as a driver. His win at the Southern 500 at Darlington in 1992 marked the beginning of a long winless streak, one that led Waltrip to sell his race team and seek employment once again as a driver.

Although his later on-track performances may be lacking, often due to the equipment he has been racing in, Darrell Waltrip is still one of the most respected figures in Winston Cup racing.

RIGHT: **Darrell Waltrip climbs from the number 1 Pennzoil stock car in 1998. Filling in for an injured Steve Park, Waltrip rejuvenated his career with top-ten finishes during that Winston Cup season.**

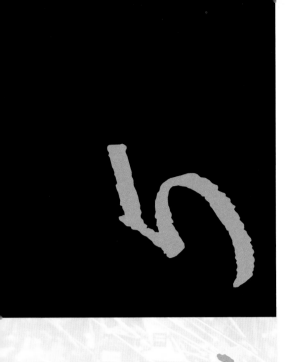

The New Wave

By the beginning of the 1990s, the Winston Cup Series had attained a level of popularity that was astonishing. And not only was the sport popular with fans, it had become a darling of the business world. Many top corporations were aware that, for the cost of a two- or three-million-dollar sponsorship, their logo would get incredible TV exposure week after week on telecasts of the Winston Cup Series. This time more than ever now that every race was broadcast live on either the traditional networks or one of several cable channels that had joined ESPN in covering NASCAR's top division.

While the schedule of the series had been relatively stable for a number of years, the popularity of NASCAR in the 1990s led to the biggest boom of new speedway construction since the 1960s. NASCAR's Winston Cup Series was becoming a national obsession, a fact that was reflected by the erection of huge new speedways like New Hampshire International Speedway, California Speedway, Texas Motor Speedway, and Las Vegas Motor Speedway.

The Winston Cup Series point fund, which amounted to a relatively humble $100,000 when founded in 1971, had skyrocketed toward the $5 million mark. A multimillion dollar bonus system for individual races was also in place, thanks to R.J. Reynolds' continuing participation in the series.

Total season attendance at Winston Cup series races by the middle of the decade was nearing six million, and the days of women having good reason to hesitate to attend a race were dim memories as fan demographics spread across all categories. Indeed, one financial publication, *Forbes,* estimated that NASCAR's gross profits were an incredible $2 billion.

Of course, it would be meaningless without strong competition, the one consistent thread that led all the way back to the first Strictly Stock race in Charlotte, North Carolina, in 1949. Perhaps the days of Tim Flock's racing monkey, Jocko Flocko, and nights of hard partying in the 1960s had given way to modern drivers carrying briefcases and conscientiously staying on their best behavior. But what really matters is that the sport of stock car racing depends on close finishes and heated rivalries, and in the 1990s, the superstars of stock car racing made it clear they were redefining the parameters of NASCAR competition.

OPPOSITE: **Derrike Cope screams along NASCAR's most famous track in front of a blur of empty stands on February 7, 1999, during Daytona Speedweek.**

ABOVE: **Davey Allison in 1988, early in his Winston Cup career. In later seasons young Allison switched to an enclosed-face crash helmet.**

Davey **Allison**

It's rare that a winning tradition can span decades, but the son of NASCAR star Bobby Allison came to the Winston Cup Series and seemed likely to carry the legend of "The Alabama Gang" into the year 2000 and beyond.

Davey Allison was surrounded by racing from the time he was born. Watching his father Bobby and uncle Donnie compete in NASCAR's top series obviously had a major impact on the young driver. By the time he was a teenager, Davey began to follow the path that leads to Winston Cup racing. Competing on local short tracks, the young Allison learned what it takes to be a racer. Like many others, he moved up to compete in Automobile Racing Club of America events, getting a taste of what it was like to compete in Winston Cup–style cars. Then came a handful of starts in Winston Cup races in 1985 and 1986. Finally, in 1987, it was time for Davey to run a full season

and try for Rookie of the Year honors. He won three races in that first season, and the newest member of the Alabama Gang was on his way.

The next season began with the 1988 Daytona 500. Davey was in contention all day, and nearly won NASCAR's biggest race. But coming in second didn't bother him that much— father Bobby was the race winner.

In 191 Winston Cup starts, Davey Allison won nineteen times. He became a fan favorite, battling side by side with Dale Earnhardt and Rusty Wallace. He nearly won the 1992 championship, losing it only when he was caught up in a crash triggered by Ernie Irvan's tire failure in the last race of the season.

It seemed that Davey would have many more opportunities to win championships, but it was not to be. In July 1993, Davey and long-time racing companion Red Farmer were flying to Talladega Superspeedway to observe a test session. While landing in the speedway infield, Davey lost control of aircraft. He died shortly after the crash. Farmer survived the accident.

As the 1990s dawned, Davey Allison looked to be one of NASCAR's greatest superstars. That he did not live to fulfill that destiny is one of racing's sadder tales.

John **Andretti**

Like his famous uncle Mario, John Andretti has had a long fascination with motorsports. But unlike Mario, who only dabbled with NASCAR racing on occasion, John has settled on Winston Cup racing as his career.

After racing in events ranging from the Indianapolis 500 to France's famed twenty-four-hour race in LeMans, Andretti made his first Winston Cup start for car owner Billy Hagan in 1993. Andretti moved to a new team founded by Michael Kranefuss and Carl Haas in 1995, winning a pole position. Midway through the 1996 season, the Kranefuss/Haas team switched drivers with Cale Yarborough's team. Jeremy

ABOVE: **Sometimes all a driver can do is wait. Here John Andretti stands ready in the garage area at Charlotte Motor Speedway as a Cale Yarborough race team crewman preps his Ford Thunderbird.**

Mayfield took over Andretti's spot, while John moved on to drive Thunderbirds for NASCAR legend Yarborough.

Yarborough's team had not been among the most competitive in the Winston Cup Series, but on July 5, 1997, Andretti held off the competition at Daytona International Speedway and won his first race on one of NASCAR's most demanding superspeedways.

In 1998, Andretti moved once again, this time driving for NASCAR's greatest hero, Richard Petty.

Jeff **Burton**

The Winston Cup Series Rookie of the Year in 1994, Jeff Burton followed the same career path as his brother Ward, starting at local tracks in his native Virginia then working his way through the Busch Grand National Series to move up to NASCAR's top division.

Jeff started his Winston Cup career with the Stavola Brothers racing team, who provided the Fords he drove to the rookie title. But Burton's strong runs attracted the eye of well-known team owner Jack Roush. Roush had first become involved in Winston Cup racing in 1987, fielding cars for Mark Martin. But Roush Racing in the 1990s was undergoing a tremendous expansion, swelling to five stock cars by 1998. As a key part of that expansion, Roush signed Burton for the 1996 season and beyond.

Veteran Mark Martin, one of NASCAR's most highly regarded drivers, hit it off with Burton and helped his teammate with advice that accelerated Jeff's learning curve tremendously.

At Texas Motor Speedway's inaugural race in 1997, while many drivers were struggling with the difficult new track, Jeff Burton drove to his first Winston Cup win. He followed that up with wins at New Hampshire International Speedway and the tough Martinsville Speedway. Teamed with experienced crew chief Buddy Parrott, Burton went on to become a consistent presence at the front of the field, with two more wins coming in the 1998 season, which was dominated by Jeff Gordon and Martin.

With the race operations of Martin and Burton located in the same complex, it's likely that some of the success that Martin experienced in 1998—including eight Winston Cup wins—will help make Burton's team even stronger.

Ward **Burton**

Ward Burton was the first of the Burton brothers to win in Winston Cup competition after both graduated to NASCAR's elite division in 1994.

Burton arrived in Winston Cup racing after winning four times in the Busch Grand National Series. His first pole came late in his rookie Winston Cup season, driving for the Dillard Motorsports team he had raced with in the Busch series. After a disappointing season, winning the pole at Charlotte Motor Speedway in October 1994 was a morale boost. But Burton would not break into victory lane until he switched teams, driving for car owner Bill Davis. In his fifty-third Winston Cup start—on October 22, 1995, at North Carolina Motor Speedway—Burton held off a determined Rusty Wallace to win for the first time in Winston Cup competition.

Derrike **Cope**

Even Derrike Cope was surprised when he won the 1990 Daytona 500. The young driver had never won in the Winston Cup Series, but he had a great run going in the February classic. With Cope racing in second place as the event neared its finish, the 500 seemed to be Dale Earnhardt's. The veteran had a fairly comfortable lead, and it seemed that after more than a decade of trying Earnhardt would win NASCAR's biggest race. But then, going toward turn three on the race's final lap, Cope saw one of Earnhardt's tires fail. Steering his Chevrolet past Dale's slowing car, Derrike Cope inherited the lead with just two turns left to negotiate. Holding off a charge by Terry Labonte, Cope found himself in the historic victory lane at Daytona International Speedway.

OPPOSITE: **Jeff (left) and Ward (right) Burton not only made it into the top NASCAR division, they have both become winners in the Winston Cup Series.** ABOVE: **Derrike Cope sits behind the wheel of the Bob Whitcomb–owned Chevrolet in 1988. When Whitcomb unexpectedly closed his racing operation in 1992, it sent Cope's successful Winston Cup career into a slump.** BELOW: **Ward Burton spins in front of a pack of cars at New Hampshire in 1998. The tire smoke from a spinning car can create a virtual white wall on the track, leaving drivers approaching the accident wondering nervously if they'll pass through unscathed.**

ABOVE: **Harry Gant loved the racing in the Winston Cup Series, but the North Carolina driver never let increasing media coverage and fan hysteria change his unpretentious nature.** OPPOSITE: **On May 1, 1983, Phil Parsons (in the 66 Skoal ride) goes end-over-end in what ultimately turned into a nine-car pileup while teammate Harry Gant (33), Bill Elliott (9), and A.J. Foyt slip through unscathed. Pole winner Cale Yarborough (28) was one of the unlucky nine.**

Cope's path to Daytona had begun in his native Washington, racing at the local Yakima racetrack. Derrike had progressed on to late-model racing and then began to race in the NASCAR Winston West division. In 1982, he first tested the Winston Cup waters, though it would take years before that first win in Daytona.

Derrike Cope followed up his Daytona 500 victory with a second win in 1990, at the tough Dover Downs International Speedway. Then, just prior to the 1993 Daytona 500, team owner Bob Whitcomb shut down his racing operation.

Derrike Cope spent much of the 1990s racing in cars that were not at a competitive advantage, but an association with Bahari Racing in 1998 found the team winning a pole position as the fastest qualifier at Charlotte Motor Speedway late in the season. It was a sign that Derrike Cope could soon be on his way to his next Winston Cup victory.

Harry **Gant**

Sports fans love winning streaks, and Harry Gant built one of NASCAR's most popular in 1991.

Gant did not start his Winston Cup career until he was in his thirties, when he made his debut driving for car owner Junie Donlavey in 1973. It took nearly ten years for Gant to win his first Winston Cup race—in April 1982 at Martinsville—although he followed that up weeks later with another win,

at Charlotte Motor Speedway. Harry came in second in the 1984 Winston Cup championship battle and showed his skills by winning the all-star International Race of Champions title in 1986.

Harry Gant continued to win at least one race per season in 1989 and 1990, but in the fall of 1991 he hit a hot streak that had the Winston Cup world buzzing. Gant won four races in a row driving his green Oldsmobile, including one in which the car was damaged in a crash. Even the accident could not stop Harry, however, and he earned the title "Mr. September" for the late-season heroics.

Harry Gant's last NASCAR Winston Cup start came at the age of fifty-five, when he returned from his 1994 retirement to substitute for an injured Bill Elliott in a race at Charlotte Motor Speedway in 1996.

Jeff **Gordon**

Just a few short years ago, most people felt that Richard Petty's incredible records from his decades-long NASCAR career would last forever. After all, the King had set some standards that certainly seemed unobtainable by modern Winston Cup drivers. Then along came a young driver from California by way of Indiana who set the NASCAR world on its ear.

Fittingly, Jeff Gordon made his first Winston Cup start in Richard Petty's final race, at Atlanta in 1992. Gordon had established himself in open-wheel racing in the Midwest before moving south to try his hand at stock car racing. He attracted much attention in the Busch Grand National Series with torrid qualifying runs and hard charges in competition.

Jeff caught the eye of Winston Cup team owner Rick Hendrick, who lured Gordon from the Ford camp to become part of his stable of three Chevrolet teams. In 1993, his first full season in Winston Cup racing, Jeff won one of the 125-mile (200km) qualifying races

OPPOSITE: **Jeff Gordon leads the charge down the straightaway at Martinsville, having gained enough of an advantage through his Lumina's power to be in position to cut in front of Rusty Wallace and claim the lead in the preferred lower groove.** ABOVE: **Racing maturity can take years to develop in the Winston Cup Series, especially when success comes early in a driver's career. But Jeff Gordon has set new standards for driver conduct in the modern high-profile NASCAR world.**

for the Daytona 500 and finished in the top five at seven races on his way to snagging Rookie of the Year honors. It was clear that it wouldn't be long before Gordon and his brilliant crew chief, Ray Evernham, would put together some wins.

Back at Daytona to start the 1994 season, Gordon won the all-star Busch Clash special event. Then, in May at Charlotte Motor Speedway's 600-mile (960km) event, Gordon tasted victory in his first Winston Cup points race win. When other drivers pitted late in NASCAR's longest race to take on four tires, Evernham gambled on taking just two tires. It was up to Gordon to hold off the other cars, and he succeeded.

Just weeks later, in NASCAR's first visit to Indianapolis Motor Speedway, Gordon won in his adopted home state at the inaugural Brickyard 400, the highest profile event of the 1994 season.

It set the stage for the 1995 season, in which Gordon won seven races on his way to his first NASCAR Winston Cup Series championship. At just twenty-four, he became the youngest winner of the title in NASCAR's modern era.

But Jeff was far from done. After narrowly losing the championship to his teammate Terry Labonte in 1996, Gordon bounced back in 1997 and claimed the title for a second time. Then in 1998, Gordon won a record-tying thirteen races on his way to a third championship. Gordon's single-season win mark tied Richard Petty's modern-era NASCAR record, set in 1975.

In his career, Petty won 200 races. Many thought that record was safe for all time. But Gordon's performances in the late 1990s have many observers wondering if it might be possible for Jeff Gordon to eclipse a mark once thought unreachable.

Bobby **Hamilton**

Many of NASCAR's best drivers have grown up around race cars, and Bobby Hamilton is no exception. His family was heavily involved in racing, even building the Winston Cup Series cars raced in the 1970s by country music star Marty Robbins.

But Bobby Hamilton was interested in finding his own racing stardom and began running on short tracks to build his skills. He eventually became track champion at Nashville Speedway. Darrell Waltrip, who had followed the same route to the Winston Cup Series, suggested Hamilton to car owner Rick Hendrick, who needed a driver to participate in action filming for the movie *Days of Thunder* in 1989. Driving a car specifically for the movie, Hamilton raced into the lead during a Winston Cup race in Phoenix.

When Hamilton entered the Winston Cup Series as an official competitor, he won Rookie of the Year in 1991. By 1995 he had graduated to driving for the King, Richard Petty. Petty Enterprises had not won a race since Richard retired in 1992, but Hamilton changed all that, returning the team to victory lane in 1996 and 1997. Joining the Morgan-McClure team in 1998, Bobby Hamilton kept winning, claiming the April race at Martinsville.

LEFT: Wearing the patch that bears Richard Petty's face means you're driving for Petty Enterprises, perhaps the most legendary of all NASCAR teams. Bobby Hamilton played a large role in making the team competitive once again in the 1990s. BELOW: Ernie Irvan stands beside the Morgan-McClure Chevrolet Lumina at Bristol International Raceway. Irvan claimed his first pole and first win driving this car at the short, high-banked speedway in Tennessee.

Ernie **Irvan**

Ernie Irvan's career in big league stock car racing began at Charlotte Motor Speedway. As it turned out, Irvan was not behind the wheel of a stock car thundering around the famed racetrack; instead, Irvan was at the track to build grandstands.

The California driver had decided that racing would be his career and had taken the risky path of moving across the country to settle in the Charlotte, North Carolina, area. Once relocated, he began the difficult task of building a name for himself in the racing hotbed.

Racing on local tracks, Ernie managed to develop enough of a reputation to get a Winston Cup ride for the first time in September 1987. Through the late 1980s, Irvan was able to place cars owned by D.K. Ulrich into top-ten finishes. These runs attracted the eye of the Morgan-McClure race team, who hired Irvan after the 1990 season had begun. Irvan knew that this Chevrolet team was capable of winning and that it was up to him to make the most of the opportunity. In August, at the rough Bristol Motor Speedway, Irvan battled Rusty Wallace in the final laps, holding off the experienced driver to win his first Winston Cup Series race.

Big things were in store for Irvan, and he won the 1991 Daytona 500, eventually finishing fifth in the championship points. Irvan capitalized on his ascension as a Winston Cup star, accepting a position with the highly regarded Robert Yates Ford team late in 1993, winning twice in the nine races he drove to finish out the season for his new car owner.

The 1994 season seemed to hold great promise. Irvan had three victories and was in the hunt for a championship by the time the Winston Cup Series arrived at Michigan International Speedway in August. But in a practice session for the race, Irvan's Thunderbird lost control and collided violently with the wall. Although Irvan nearly died from his injuries, he struggled through a demanding rehabilitation program, determined to return to Winston Cup racing. On October 1, 1995, he did. Irvan went on to win with Yates in both 1996 and 1997, then moved on to the MB2 Motorsports team in 1998.

Although the MB2 team was fairly new to Winston Cup racing, Ernie Irvan's experience brought them pole positions and respect and made them legitimate contenders to win in 1999 and beyond.

Dale **Jarrett**

Another member of NASCAR's next generation club, Dale Jarrett followed his father Ned into stock car racing and has become one of the sport's modern superstars.

A talented golfer, Jarrett gave up the clubs for the steering wheel and made his Winston Cup Series debut in 1987, ten years after he began racing at the highly competitive Hickory Motor Speedway in the Sportsman division. Working his way up through the NASCAR ranks, Jarrett was well-prepared for a Winston Cup career.

Driving for the highly regarded Wood Brothers team in 1991, Dale won his first Winston Cup Series race at Michigan International Speedway. He did it in grand fashion, keeping cool despite a hard charge by Davey Allison, the two cars crossing the finish line side-by-side with Jarrett ahead by mere inches.

Jarrett moved on to drive for a team owned by National Football League coach Joe Gibbs, where he outdueled Dale Earnhardt to win the 1993 Daytona 500. By 1995, Jarrett was racing for the Robert Yates Ford team, first substituting for the injured Ernie Irvan, then driving for a new Yates team headed by rising young crew chief Todd Parrott. The new team captured the 1996 Daytona 500, as well as the third running of the Brickyard 400 at Indianapolis Motor Speedway.

In 1998, Dale Jarrett put together three wins but more importantly was a

ABOVE: **Dale Jarrett's first Winston Cup win came while driving a Thunderbird for the Wood Brothers Ford team, sponsored by Citgo. It was to be his first of many wins in NASCAR's top division.**

key factor in the Winston Cup Series championship battle. Jarrett's third-place standing in the season-long quest indicates potential for Dale to win his own championship, just as his father Ned did in the 1960s.

Alan **Kulwicki**

It's an old cliché: winning takes hard work. But nothing could be more true in the world of racing. And in the Winston Cup Series, the embodiment of hard work was Alan Kulwicki.

Kulwicki began racing in the Midwest, eventually graduating to the American Speed Association stock car

OPPOSITE: **That the late Alan Kulwicki was able to beat the better-funded Winston Cup teams to win the 1992 championship was due in no small part to the driver's hands-on approach to race team ownership. His engineering degree also helped give him a competitive edge.** ABOVE: **Bobby Labonte sports a flamboyant helmet in this 1992 photograph (taken prior to competition in the Busch Series), but his winning reputation in Winston Cup racing has been built on quiet determination.**

series, as had such other Winston Cup drivers as Mark Martin and Rusty Wallace. But Alan had also devoted attention to his education, and obtained a bachelor's degree in mechanical engineering.

Moving south, Kulwicki made his first Winston Cup start in 1985. In 1986, he acquired minimal sponsorship and ran the season with just two full-time crew members and a single car. Under circumstances that many would consider hopeless from a competitive standpoint, Alan won the Rookie of the Year title. After hiring Paul Andrews as his crew chief (on the advice of Rusty Wallace), Kulwicki won his first Winston Cup race in 1988 at Phoenix. By 1992, Kulwicki was a consistent threat to win any race. He won twice that season, and in the final race of the year won the Winston Cup Series championship. He did so in that race in Atlanta by leading the most laps, then finishing second behind championship rival Bill Elliott. The runner-up finish, combined with the points bonus for laps

led, gave Alan the title over Elliott by just 10 points. Kulwicki and Andrews calculated what they needed to do while the race was under way, an example of how aware Alan and his team were of what had to be accomplished. On the day he won the championship, Alan Kulwicki's Thunderbird bore the legend "Underbird" across its front grille.

On April 1, 1993, flying to the Winston Cup Series race in Bristol, Tennessee, the plane carrying Alan Kulwicki suffered engine failure. Alan and four others died in the crash, a tragic loss for the sport.

Bobby **Labonte**

When your brother is a Winston Cup Series champion, you'd better have plenty of talent yourself if you've chosen racing as your career. But Bobby Labonte's Winston Cup record is already an enviable one, and he may very well one day have his own Winston Cup championship trophy.

Bobby followed his brother Terry's path to the heights of NASCAR, beginning by racing quarter midgets in Texas. His natural ability led to the Busch Grand National Series in 1990, where he was voted Most Popular Driver in his rookie season. The next season, though, Labonte managed an even better title: Busch Series champion. He nearly repeated the feat in 1992, before entering Winston Cup competition in 1993.

Driving for team owner Bill Davis, Bobby Labonte developed a consistent style not unlike that of his brother Terry. His runs impressed Joe Gibbs, the former National Football League coach who had founded a top Winston Cup team. When Gibbs lost driver Dale Jarrett to the Robert Yates team, he signed Bobby Labonte to replace him for 1995. Labonte rewarded Gibbs' confidence in his abilities by winning three times in their debut season together. With crew chief Jimmy Makar handling preparation and strategy, Bobby Labonte has driven the team's cars to at least one win in each season.

Sterling **Marlin**

It's hard to win any Winston Cup race. It's even harder to win the Daytona 500. But in 1994, Sterling Marlin won the Daytona 500, his very first Winston Cup Series victory—and he repeated the feat in 1995.

Marlin is the son of respected former NASCAR driver "Coo Coo" Marlin and naturally grew up around racing. Sterling showed he had great talent by winning the late model championship at Nashville Speedway in 1980, 1981, and 1982—the same competitive track that has helped build the careers of drivers like Darrell Waltrip and Bobby Hamilton.

His success on short tracks demonstrated, Marlin moved on to run with the Winston Cup Series full time in 1983. Driving for Roger Hamby, Sterling won the Rookie of the Year title and seemed to be on his way. But then season after season passed, and Marlin's first win proved to be frustratingly elusive. Even two years driving for Junior Johnson did not yield a first-place finish.

LEFT: **Sterling Marlin shares the moment with his father, Coo Coo Marlin, holding the winner's trophy after winning the Daytona 500 in 1995.** BELOW: **Mark Martin soaks up the sun at California Speedway on June 20, 1997, during the qualifying races for the California 500.**

Then Marlin joined Virginia's Morgan-McClure team, and in their very first race together, NASCAR's most important event of the season was theirs—Marlin held off Ernie Irvan's Ford to win the 1994 Daytona 500. Sterling Marlin scored three victories in 1995, and two more in 1996 before signing with team owner Felix Sabates.

Mark **Martin**

When the subjects of determination and dedication come up in Winston Cup conversation, Mark Martin's name will often be the first heard.

Martin raced in the American Speed Association series, learning the skills of stock car racing while setting his sights on the Winston Cup Series. He was ASA champion in 1978, 1979, and 1980 and seemed ready to run in NASCAR. But things did not go as planned, and after racing with limited success in fifty-one Winston Cup races between 1981 and 1983, Martin returned to ASA racing.

Winning another ASA title in 1986 was nice, but Martin refused to let his Winston Cup dream die. He returned to NASCAR's top series in 1988, driving for new team owner Jack Roush. Buoyed by ten top-ten finishes that season, Mark was ready to step up, winning his first Winston Cup race in October 1989, at North Carolina Motor Speedway. In 1990, Mark won three more races, and made a run at the Winston Cup Series championship. He fell just short, a handful of points behind Dale Earnhardt. Still, it was a remarkable run for a team that was still learning about Winston Cup racing.

The combination of Martin and Roush has been consistent, and Mark has scored multiple wins every season with the exception of 1996. He has placed second in the Winston Cup championship battle twice more, in 1994 and 1998. Since 1990, his championship standing at the end of the season has never been lower than sixth.

In 1998, Martin had a season that, while exceptional on the racetrack, was darkened by the death of his father in a plane crash. Mark also was suffering from a painful back problem that dogged him all season. Despite that, Mark won eight races and had consistent runs that ordinarily would have been good enough to win the championship. Unfortunately for the Roush team, Jeff Gordon had an astounding season, scoring thirteen wins and the season title. But Mark Martin is not one to give up, and no one would be surprised if this driver has his own championship trophy in the near future.

Jeremy **Mayfield**

Growing up in Kentucky, Jeremy Mayfield's NASCAR hero was Darrell Waltrip. It was the realization of a dream when Mayfield found himself racing with the legendary Winston Cup driver in the 1990s.

Through his teenage years Mayfield competed in a variety of motorsports classes, from go-karts to street stocks. His talent was undeniable, and in 1993 he entered into Automobile Racing Club of America competition. The ARCA stock cars are often Winston Cup cars that have been sold by race teams building new race cars, and the series races are run on many of the same superspeedways used by the Winston Cup Series. Racing on these tracks

ABOVE: **As soon as Kentucky's Jeremy Mayfield landed a ride with a high-profile race team backed by a major sponsor—and became a teammate of veteran Rusty Wallace—the young driver began to fully demonstrate his talent.**

Kyle **Petty**

Kyle Petty, the son of "King" Richard Petty and grandson of NASCAR pioneer Lee Petty, had a monumental tradition to live up to when he decided to try his hand at stock car racing. After all, Lee and Richard had accounted for much of stock car racing's history and had made contributions to NASCAR's record book that may very well be secure for all time.

But Kyle showed that the family talent had not skipped a generation

provides a young driver with the opportunity to build a background that will prove invaluable in NASCAR's elite series, and Mayfield made the most of his educational opportunities. The young driver swept ARCA Rookie of the Year honors and alerted the Winston Cup world that a potential new star had arrived.

One of those who noticed Mayfield's performances was Cale Yarborough, one of NASCAR's greatest drivers, who had fielded stock cars in the Winston Cup Series since his retirement from competition in 1988. Yarborough selected Mayfield to drive for his team in 1994. Although Jeremy still had much to learn,

he helped Yarborough's team become competitive, scoring top-five finishes in 1996. Late in that season, he joined the Michael Kranefuss-owned Ford team.

Aligned with the Penske South team of driver Rusty Wallace, Mayfield put the Kranefuss Ford car into the thick of the points race early in 1998, although his first victory still proved elusive. Then, in his 125th Winston Cup Series start, Jeremy Mayfield won at Pocono International Raceway on June 21, 1998. That win, and his strong runs throughout the season, indicate that Jeremy Mayfield is realizing the potential he has shown in his climb to NASCAR's most prestigious level.

when he made his first start in Automobile Racing Club of America competition. Racing at Daytona in February, 1979, Kyle climbed behind the wheel of his Winston Cup–like ARCA stock car and zoomed around the imposing Daytona International Speedway to win in his first super-speedway start.

The next stop for Kyle was the Winston Cup Series, where his family had had such a tremendous impact. But success for Kyle did not come as quickly or as easily as it did for the other Pettys. After racing for Petty Enterprises through 1984, Kyle decided that the family racing operation was behind the times and

left to drive for Virginia's fabled Wood Brothers team. Still, it would not be until 1986 that Kyle would win his first Winston Cup race. The win at Richmond came seven years after his first Winston Cup race.

Kyle's career since has included a long association with owner Felix Sabates. Petty later returned to Level

OPPOSITE: **Kyle Petty, the third generation of the racing Petty family. With his colorful personality, Kyle has already laid the groundwork for a career in motorsports broadcasting when he hangs up his helmet.** BELOW: **The Petty Enterprises crew in action at Pocono International Raceway. The "Petty blue" color on a Winston Cup stock car has come to symbolize the traditions of NASCAR.**

Cross, North Carolina, to drive for a second Petty Enterprises team. Through 1998, Kyle had won eight times in Winston Cup competition.

Like his father, though, Kyle Petty has become well known for his activities off the race track. Extremely active in charity work, Petty was named NASCAR's Man of the Year in 1998.

Mike **Skinner**

When NASCAR raced in Japan in November 1995, it marked the first time that Winston Cup cars raced in a NASCAR-sanctioned event so far from Daytona Beach. But the annual excursion to Japan became a highlight of the racing season, even if the races were considered exhibitions and did not count as points events. Truth be told, many of NASCAR's finest had trouble adapting to the Japanese world, but not Mike Skinner.

Skinner, who began his rookie Winston Cup career in 1997 by winning the pole for the Daytona 500, won the 1997 Japan event on a modified road course at Suzuka Circuitland. He backed up that victory in 1998, winning at the new oval track known as Twin Ring Motegi Superspeedway in Motegi City, Japan, holding off a determined charge from Jeff Gordon late in the race's closing laps. Clearly, racing 14,000 miles (22,400km) from home does not bother Skinner.

The California-born driver began his NASCAR career after his wife urged that he get serious about his career and move east to the hotbed of racing in North Carolina. Skinner's big break came when Richard Childress hired him to drive his truck in the 1995 debut season of the NASCAR Supertruck series, and Skinner rewarded Childress' faith by claiming the series title. When Childress decided to expand his Winston Cup operation by fielding a car in addition to Dale Earnhardt's number 3, Skinner got the call.

LEFT: **Bristol Motor Speedway may be the toughest of the Winston Cup venues, a short track where the cars still run laps that average more than 125 mph (200kph). Trouble can strike with absolutely no warning on the tight oval, as Mike Skinner in the 31 car and Chad Little have just discovered.** ABOVE: **Mike Skinner has suffered from injuries sustained in brutal crashes early in the 1998 and 1999 Winston Cup seasons. Overcoming these obstacles, he has risen to NASCAR stardom.**

Skinner was injured in a devastating crash at Atlanta Motor Speedway early in the 1998 season, and his physical problems hampered his on-track efforts. But as Skinner healed his finishes improved, helped by the presence of crew chief Larry McReynolds, who moved to the team from the Earnhardt operation in mid-season. Skinner showed strength on the superspeedways, finishing third at Daytona late in the season.

With McReynolds in place as crew chief for 1999, Mike Skinner is poised to become one of Winston Cup racing's superstars.

OPPOSITE: **Jimmy Spencer roars along at Talladega in 1994, on his way to his second Winston Cup win of the season. Some drivers are uncomfortable at the huge superspeedways, but Spencer has perfected the art of racing on NASCAR's fastest tracks.** ABOVE: **NASCAR has built its reputation on close finishes: Jimmy Spencer is seen enjoying victory lane in 1994 after winning his first race in one of the Winston Cup Series' most exciting sprints to the finish line. Spencer outdueled Ernie Irvan in a superspeedway showdown at Daytona.**

Jimmy **Spencer**

In an era when it is not uncommon to see a NASCAR Winston Cup Series driver arrive in the garage area carefully dressed and with briefcase in tow, nicknames for colorful behavior have become harder to come by. But when Pennsylvania's Jimmy Spencer arrived in the Winston Cup Series, his nickname was already in place—Mister Excitement.

Spencer had gained that name for his hard charges in short track competition, and the name was reinforced after he moved on to compete in

NASCAR's tough Modified series. He brought the Modified sensibility of hard charging with him when he moved south to compete in the Busch Grand National Series.

Spencer was thrilled when former driver Buddy Baker offered him a chance to drive his Winston Cup car in 1989. Other drivers in the series were not too thrilled when they encountered Spencer's aggressive approach to racing in NASCAR's top series.

But over time, Jimmy Spencer learned when to charge hard and when to take care of his equipment. Much of the education resulted from driving for former

NASCAR greats like Baker, Bobby Allison, and Junior Johnson. Indeed, it was while driving for Johnson that Spencer won his first Winston Cup pole and race. In a thrilling side-by-side battle at Daytona's July race in 1994, Spencer set up a brilliant strategy and edged ahead of Ernie Irvan for his first win.

Spencer won a second race in 1994, at the Talladega Superspeedway. Superspeedway racing, with its high speeds and dramatic close-quarters racing, seems uniquely suited to Jimmy Spencer's talents, and he will often be found at the front of the pack on NASCAR's biggest race tracks.

Into the Crystal Ball

As NASCAR's celebration of its first fifty years ended with the last race of the 1998 season, many of stock car racing's fans and observers were facing a troubling question: Had the slow, methodical growth of a sport carefully cultivating itself for a place in the national eye been replaced by a headlong rush for money, fueled by the greed of wealthy track owners and souvenir corporations? It was a question that seemed valid.

Fan outrage seemed to be growing, generally stirred up by new ticket policies and higher prices. Some tracks required fans to purchase licenses for the privilege of buying seats, while others required fans to buy tickets for every race the track hosts, not just the Winston Cup Series events. These restrictive policies were often accompanied by skyrocketing ticket prices. Some fans felt they had been priced out of the sport that they had helped build, the loyalty of decades betrayed by the hunger for the quick buck.

And as the tracks sought to increase revenues, long-time fans found new grandstands that in many cases completely surrounded the racetracks. With those grandstands came tens of thousands of new fans, more traffic,

increasingly hard-to-find accommodations, and all of the other "benefits" of NASCAR being crowned America's hot sport.

Every week when the field took the green flag, it seemed that at least a few of the cars were sporting special "commemorative" paint jobs—honoring an anniversary, advertising a new feature film, or just providing a different look. Of course, for every car that raced under special colors, thousands of metal die-cast models went on sale to the race fans. Whereas at the beginning of the decade a fan could quite easily afford every 1/24th scale die-cast car released by the handful of companies in the business, by 1998 the deluge of little cars was dizzying. The sum required to buy one of each would have been astonishing, not to mention the space a collector would have to have to store the bounty.

Even the race teams themselves encountered financial concerns. The cost of a top-notch corporate sponsorship had swollen to $6 to $8 million per season, and many companies balked at the astronomical figures. Worse, there were more race teams than there were starting spots in the races themselves, and that meant there were unhappy sponsors left in the lurch as unfortunate

OPPOSITE: **With racing in his blood, Dale Earnhardt, Jr., is the consummate representative of the new generation of up-and-coming NASCAR superstars. Here he tips his hat to the crowd on October 4, 1998.**

race teams were sent home. At the end of the year, a number of well-established teams were forced out of business.

But aside from the dim business aspects of the 1998 season, there was one concern that was particularly disturbing—simply stated, many of the races in what was supposed to have been NASCAR's most glorious season were boring. Jeff Gordon's Chevrolet Monte Carlo was the championship class of the field, easily fending off a gallant challenge by Mark Martin in his Ford Taurus. But while the championship battle was at least reasonably interesting, the races themselves all too often were not. Martin and Gordon won twenty of the races, and in many cases the car that was the strongest at a particular racetrack went to the front of the field early in an event and was never challenged.

As a result, some crucial television ratings were disappointing, and, in an especially alarming development, empty rows of seats in the grandstands were visible on the broadcasts of some of the races.

Not that the season was totally lackluster. To be sure, NASCAR's fiftieth season did have its highlights. The season began on a tremendously high note when Dale Earnhardt finally won his Daytona 500, after twenty years of failure. "My eyes watered up in the race car," the great warrior admitted, and many fans were equally touched.

Another highlight was the incredibly gutsy performance of Ricky Rudd, struggling to keep his streak of at least one victory per season intact. On a blistering hot day Martinsville Speedway, Rudd's driver cooling system failed in the race's early laps. "I told the crew, 'You need to line up a relief driver. This seat is absolutely burning me up.'" But Rudd couldn't get out of the car—after a long season of disappointing runs, his Ford was the strongest of all the cars challenging the tough short track in Virginia. Despite the blistering of his skin and severe dehydration, Rudd raced on to victory. It was the kind of performance that creates legends.

When NASCAR settled in at New York's Waldorf Astoria for its annual Winston Cup Series awards banquet, NASCAR president Bill France, Jr., was armed with statistics that painted a rosy picture of the sport's health. He boasted that NASCAR's television ratings were second only to the NFL among sporting events, even while acknowledging the troubling notions of certain race teams going out of business.

"It costs money to go fast. To go faster it costs more money," France said. "If the costs go too high, that excitement will disappear. The good news is that NASCAR racing is relatively affordable, and that has kept competition close."

Further helping the competition is new talent that is drawn to the Winston Cup Series. As NASCAR enters its

BELOW: Racing in the Busch Grand National Series teaches a young driver how to race in NASCAR's major leagues. Here Dale Earnhardt, Jr., learns how not to make a pit stop.

ABOVE: **Dale Earnhardt, Jr., first raced against his legendary father in an exhibition race in Japan after the 1998 Winston Cup season, as the young driver prepared to make his official Winston Cup debut in the 1999 season.**

second fifty years, a new crop of drivers are either entering the premier NASCAR series or are poised to do so after cutting their teeth in the ASA, ARCA, and NASCAR Busch Grand National and Craftsman Truck Series.

As long as NASCAR's Winston Cup Series remains U.S. racing's top attraction, great young drivers will long to compete against the legends of stock car racing. Here are some drivers expected to make their own mark on the record books of NASCAR in the decades to come.

Dale **Earnhardt, Jr.**

If proof is needed of the family heritage of young Dale Earnhardt, Jr., just consider the fact that his nickname in the NASCAR world is simply "Junior." When everybody knows your father is a seven-time Winston Cup champion, Junior is all you need.

When Junior makes his Winston Cup debut in 1999 at five select races, it will be one of the most highly anticipated debuts in racing. There is no doubting this young driver's talent;

the son of Dale Earnhardt and grandson of NASCAR pioneer Ralph Earnhardt had cut a path through short tracks of the South before arriving in the NASCAR Busch Grand National Series with a handful of starts in 1997. In 1998, Junior made a concerted effort in running the entire Busch Series schedule. Considering his family tree, the results of Junior's Busch Series assault should not be too surprising—seven wins, sixteen top-five finishes, and the Busch Grand National championship. But it's all the more impressive when you consider that much of Junior's success came on tracks that he had never raced on before.

In November 1998, the Earnhardts Junior and Senior competed against each other at the Twin Ring Motegi Superspeedway in Japan. In the exhibition race, the two raced side-by-side on occasion. But at the end of the race, young Dale beat out his father, finishing sixth to Dale Senior's eighth-place finish.

With Dale Earnhardt, Jr., scheduled to test the Winston Cup waters in 1999 and run a full season in 2000, many competitors in NASCAR's top division are already concerned that the fruits of Junior's accelerated learning curve will come at their expense.

Ron **Hornaday**

For a driver trying to make a good impression in the racing community, it's important to perform well. But there's even more pressure when your team owner is NASCAR's legendary "Intimidator," Dale Earnhardt. Though Ron Hornaday has faced such pressure in his career driving in the NASCAR Craftsman Truck Series for Earnhardt, he has actually thrived on the expectations that go along with such a high-profile job.

Hornaday attracted Earnhardt's attention running on the West Coast in NASCAR's regional Southwest Tour. Hornaday was a two-time champion in the series, and, with some of the series races broadcast on television, Hornaday's name began to crop up in racing conversations.

When Earnhardt hired him to drive his truck in the 1995 inaugural season of the Craftsman Truck Series, Hornaday repaid Dale's confidence by driving to four poles and six victories. He won the same number of races in 1996, but added the series championship to his list of achievements. Hornaday managed to up his win total to seven in 1997, but fell just short in the championship battle. Determined to reclaim the title in 1998, Hornaday staged a fierce season-long battle with

ABOVE: **Ron Hornaday behind the wheel of his NASCAR Supertruck. The construction of the racing trucks is not all that different from the vehicles of NASCAR's stock car series.**

fellow competitor Jack Sprague. The championship came down to the final race. Though Sprague won the event, Hornaday finished right behind his rival in second place, which was good enough to give Ron the championship by just three points.

Ron Hornaday's aggressive-but-intelligent charges in the Craftsman Truck Series have attracted considerable attention among Winston Cup team owners, and it would surprise no one to see him become equally successful in NASCAR's toughest division.

Buckshot Jones

With a colorful name that would be right at home in accounts of NASCAR racing of the 1950s and 1960s, Buckshot Jones has proven that he has a temperament that would not have been out of place in NASCAR's legendary rough-and-tumble days.

Jones first won in the Busch Grand National Series in 1997, following a path that he and his father hoped would lead them to the Winston Cup Series. A second Busch win in 1998 didn't hurt, but perhaps more impressive was Jones' performance in a Winston Cup race at Dover, Delaware, on May 31, 1998. As part of Jones' long-term Winston Cup plans, the young driver hoped to make the field in several 1998 races for NASCAR's top series. At Dover, not only did Jones make the field, but he drove away with an eighth-place finish in what was just his second Winston Cup start. It was an eye-opening performance that got the Winston Cup garage area buzzing.

But the Busch Grand National garage was buzzing in 1998 about a series of on-track incidents between Jones and Busch series champion Randy Lajoie. Bad blood between the two led to several Busch Grand National races

ABOVE: **Buckshot Jones began campaigning in earnest in Winston Cup events during the 1999 season. Though top-ten finishes were a long shot for the young driver and his team, they did frequently qualify to race—a real achievement when there are often fifty teams competing for forty starting spots.** LEFT: **Buckshot Jones leads the way off a turn at Charlotte Motor Speedway in 1997. Jones' aggressive charges led to a fierce rivalry with fellow Busch Series driver Randy Lajoie.**

where the two drivers appeared to take each other out of competition.

Buckshot Jones' talent is unquestioned, but many observers are waiting to see if Jones will be able to temper his aggression and learn the patience necessary for success in the NASCAR Winston Cup Series.

ABOVE: **Matt Kenseth (left) chats with one of Mark Martin's crewmen at Charlotte Motor Speedway. Kenseth would do well to plan on getting to know the Winston Cup garage area, for his first runs in NASCAR's senior series have been quite successful.**

Matt **Kenseth**

It's known as the "Monster Mile"—Dover Downs International Speedway, a treacherous one-mile (1.6km) oval with high banks in the turns and an unforgiving concrete surface. More than one Winston Cup driver will admit that racing at Dover can be extremely difficult. But in September 1998, young Matt Kenseth traveled to Delaware and nearly tamed the monster.

Kenseth had already attracted attention among Winston Cup car owners, winning his first Busch Grand National Series race in just his twenty-fourth start. So when Bill Elliott's father passed away just before the Winston Cup circuit was to race at Dover, Kenseth got a last-minute offer to

climb behind the wheel of Elliott's Ford. With little practice, Kenseth qualified the car in sixteenth place. Then on Sunday, Kenseth ran Elliott's car in the lead pack all day, racing alongside the likes of Jeff Gordon and Mark Martin. When the checkered flag fell, Kenseth had completed his debut at one of NASCAR's roughest tracks with an impressive sixth-place finish. For good measure, he had won the Busch race the previous day.

Kenseth wrapped up his 1998 Busch campaign finishing second in points behind champion Dale Earnhardt, Jr., just 48 points back. Regardless, in a season when many young drivers showed potential, Matt Kenseth made it clear that he has what it takes to succeed in Winston Cup racing.

Adam **Petty**

In 1998, eighteen-year-old Adam Petty began living up to the exceptionally high standards set by his forebears.

Of course, the name Petty is synonymous with stock car racing. Adam's father Kyle is a Winston Cup star with multiple wins, Kyle's father Richard set many NASCAR records that may never be broken, and Richard's father Lee was one of the sports founders and toughest competitors. That left Adam with some mighty big footsteps to follow in.

Adam began the 1998 season racing in the American Speed Association series, the same series that gave drivers like Mark Martin, Rusty Wallace, and Alan Kulwicki their start. Adam not only grabbed a pole in his first year

RIGHT: **Busch Series wins attract the attention of Winston Cup team owners looking for new talent. Elliott Sadler went from being track champion in South Boston, Virginia, to Busch Series wins like this one at Rockingham in 1998—and in 1999 he landed the coveted assignment of driver for the famed Wood Brothers Winston Cup team.** BELOW: **Three generations of the Petty family celebrate the first ARCA win for young Adam Petty at Charlotte Motor Speedway in 1998. Adam is flanked by grandfather Richard on the left and father Kyle on the right.**

of ASA competition, but the young driver claimed a victory. But the biggest highlight was yet to come.

Moving up to the Automobile Racing Club of America series, and racing in cars nearly identical to the Winston Cup cars, Adam made his debut at Charlotte Motor Speedway in October. When father Kyle made his ARCA debut in 1979, he won his very first race. Like father, like son—young Adam held off a charge by veteran Mike Wallace to win his debut in the series and stake a claim to future greatness.

Not all of Adam's first year in professional racing was perfect—he was visited by tragedy when a freak pit road accident resulted in the loss of the life of his ASA crew chief, Chris Bradley.

But, all too often, dealing with tragedy is a part of racing, and Adam's win at Charlotte proved that he was fast becoming a true champion.

Elliott **Sadler**

Virginia has contributed many of racing's greatest names, from Elmo Langley to Ricky Rudd. Soon the Virginia hall of fame may very well include the name Elliott Sadler.

Elliott's brother, Hermie, made the leap to NASCAR's Busch Grand National Series in 1993. Younger brother Elliott was quickly learning the racing ropes, though, taking over where his brother left off with victories and track championships at the famed South Boston, Virginia, short track. On the

high-speed, tight turns of this famous little track, Elliott learned skills that would soon serve him well when he made his own move to the NASCAR Busch series in 1997.

When he arrived in the Busch series, he soon proved he was ready to win, and win he did, making a run at the series championship while he was at it. The strong rookie performance, and powerful runs in 1998, soon caught the eye of some Winston Cup luminaries. Elliott's talent was recognized by the Wood Brothers, a Virginian racing team whose record is one of the Winston Cup Series' finest. After a disappointing relationship with driver Michael Waltrip, the Wood Brothers gambled on young Elliott Sadler for the 1999 season.

Drivers who are rookies in the Winston Cup Series go through an inevitable learning period, resulting in mistakes and cars that need to be repaired in the wake of those mistakes. But Elliott's flashes of brilliance that lit up the Busch Series convinced the Wood Brothers that Elliott has what it takes to become a NASCAR Winston Cup Series star.

Jack **Sprague**

Jack Sprague has been a mainstay of NASCAR's truck racing series in recent years, and he couldn't ask for a better team owner than Rick Hendrick.

Sprague first began to make waves in NASCAR when he raced in the Busch Grand National Series in the early 1990s, with more than seventy starts to his credit. But, like many young drivers trying to establish their name, Jack saw the opportunity presented by NASCAR's move toward sanctioning a series dedicated to modified pickup truck racing.

ABOVE: **Jack Sprague is a top contender for the NASCAR Supertruck Series championship every season. His smart racing strategy and strong runs have attracted a lot of attention in the world of Winston Cup racing.** BELOW: **Elliott Sadler in the 66 car leads the field onto the track in Busch Grand National competition at Texas Motor Speedway in 1998. Racing well on tracks that the Winston Cup Series competes on helps build a solid skill set for the move to NASCAR's top series.**

ABOVE: **Though he has entered the realm of Winston Cup racing, Tony Stewart's dream of winning the Indianapolis 500 is still a driving force in his life.**

1998 NASCAR Craftsman Truck Series champion, battling down to the season's final race with rival Ron Hornaday. Sprague finished in the runner-up position by just three points, despite winning the final race.

Many feel that Jack Sprague has the talent to succeed in the Winston Cup Series, and that Hendrick Motorsports could very well help him make the transition from the truck series to NASCAR's top series.

Tony **Stewart**

Driver Tony Stewart reflects an increasingly common career path in U.S. automobile racing.

Stewart had proven he has racing ability on the track and the media skills necessary to succeed off the track. He had honed the necessities competing in open wheel racing and making a name for himself as an intelligent racer. Along the way Stewart competed in the Indianapolis 500, and became the 1997 Indy Racing League champion. At one time, a young driver with this talent would have been expected to continue to cultivate an open wheel career. But the wild popularity of stock car racing now makes NASCAR racing the goal of almost every young race car driver in the United States.

To realize that goal, Tony Stewart was fortunate to have his talent noticed by former Washington Redskins coach Joe Gibbs. Gibbs was already fielding a single-car Winston Cup team with driver Bobby Labonte. But noticing the trend toward multicar teams, Gibbs signed Stewart to compete in the Busch Grand National Series in 1997 and 1998, with a move to the Winston Cup level planned for 1999.

Tony Stewart gained invaluable experience running in the Busch series, mastering the sometimes difficult transition from open wheel race cars to stock cars. Whether he will master the Winston Cup Series as well, and become one of NASCAR's superstars, remains to be seen.

Late in 1995, Sprague competed in the final portion of the truck series schedule driving for Hendrick Motorsports. He got his feet wet in seven races that year, setting the stage for a most successful 1996 that saw Sprague win five times. In 1997, Sprague continued his winning ways by claiming three races and the series championship. He nearly repeated as

Bibliography

Fielden, Greg. *Forty Years of Stock Car Racing*, vols. 1–4. Surfside Beach, South Carolina: Galfield Press, 1990

————. *Forty Years of Stock Car Racing: Forty Plus Four*. Surfside Beach, South Carolina: Galfield Press, 1994

———— and Peter Golenbock. *Stock Car Racing Encyclopedia*. New York: Macmillan, 1997

Gilliam, George. *Racin'*. Charlottesville, Virginia: Howell Press, 1988

Girdler, Allan. *Stock Car Racers*. Osceola, Wisconsin: Motorbooks International, 1988

Moriarty, Frank. *Sunday Drivers: NASCAR Winston Cup Stock Car Racing*. Charlottesville, Virginia: Howell Press, 1994

————. *Supercars*. Charlottesville, Virginia: Howell Press, 1995

————. *The Encyclopedia of Stock Car Racing*. New York: Metrobooks, 1998

Parsons, Benny. *Inside Track*. New York: Artisan, 1996

Various. *American Racing Classics*. Concord, North Carolina: Griggs Publishing, 1992–94

————. *NASCAR Winston Cup Series Media Guide*. Winston-Salem, North Carolina: Sports Marketing Enterprises, various seasons

Yates, Brock. *The Great Drivers*. Nashville, Tennessee: Opryland USA, 1984

Appendix

NASCAR WINSTON CUP CHAMPIONS (INCLUDING GRAND NATIONAL CHAMPIONS, 1949–1970)

YEAR	DRIVER	CAR MAKE	WINS	POLES	YEAR	DRIVER	CAR MAKE	WINS	POLES
1949	Red Byron	Oldsmobile	2	1	1974	Richard Petty	Dodge	9	7
1950	Bill Rexford	Oldsmobile	1	0	1975	Richard Petty	Dodge	13	3
1951	Herb Thomas	Hudson	7	4	1976	Cale Yarborough	Chevrolet	9	2
1952	Tim Flock	Hudson	8	4	1977	Cale Yarborough	Chevrolet	9	3
1953	Herb Thomas	Hudson	11	10	1978	Cale Yarborough	Oldsmobile	10	8
1954	Lee Petty	Chrysler	7	3	1979	Richard Petty	Chevrolet	5	1
1955	Tim Flock	Chrysler	18	19	1980	Dale Earnhardt	Chevrolet	5	0
1956	Buck Baker	Chrysler	14	12	1981	Darrell Waltrip	Buick	12	11
1957	Buck Baker	Chevrolet	10	5	1982	Darrell Waltrip	Buick	12	7
1958	Lee Petty	Oldsmobile	7	4	1983	Bobby Allison	Buick	6	0
1959	Lee Petty	Plymouth	10	2	1984	Terry Labonte	Chevrolet	2	2
1960	Rex White	Chevrolet	6	3	1985	Darrell Waltrip	Chevrolet	3	4
1961	Ned Jarrett	Chevrolet	1	4	1986	Dale Earnhardt	Chevrolet	5	1
1962	Joe Weatherly	Pontiac	9	6	1987	Dale Earnhardt	Chevrolet	11	1
1963	Joe Weatherly	Mercury	3	6	1988	Bill Elliott	Ford	6	6
1964	Richard Petty	Plymouth	9	8	1989	Rusty Wallace	Pontiac	6	4
1965	Ned Jarrett	Ford	13	9	1990	Dale Earnhardt	Chevrolet	9	4
1966	David Pearson	Dodge	14	7	1991	Dale Earnhardt	Chevrolet	4	0
1967	Richard Petty	Plymouth	27	18	1992	Alan Kulwicki	Ford	2	6
1968	David Pearson	Ford	16	12	1993	Dale Earnhardt	Chevrolet	6	2
1969	David Pearson	Ford	11	14	1994	Dale Earnhardt	Chevrolet	4	2
1970	Bobby Isaac	Dodge	11	13	1995	Jeff Gordon	Chevrolet	7	8
1971	Richard Petty	Plymouth	21	9	1996	Terry Labonte	Chevrolet	2	4
1972	Richard Petty	Plymouth	8	3	1997	Jeff Gordon	Chevrolet	10	1
1973	Benny Parsons	Chevrolet	1	0	1998	Jeff Gordon	Chevrolet	13	7

WINSTON CUP SERIES ROOKIES OF THE YEAR

YEAR	DRIVERS	RACES	WINS	TOP 5	POLES
1971	Walter Ballard	41	0	3	0
1972	Larry Smith	23	0	0	0
1973	Lennie Pond	23	0	1	0
1974	Earl Ross	21	1	5	0
1975	Bruce Hill	26	0	3	0
1976	Skip Manning	27	0	0	0
1977	Ricky Rudd	25	0	1	0
1978	Ronnie Thomas	27	0	0	0
1979	Dale Earnhardt	27	1	11	4
1980	Jody Ridley	31	0	2	0
1981	Ron Bouchard	22	1	5	1
1982	Geoff Bodine	25	0	4	2
1983	Sterling Marlin	30	0	0	0
1984	Rusty Wallace	30	0	2	0
1985	Ken Schrader	28	0	0	0
1986	Alan Kulwicki	23	0	1	0
1987	Davey Allison	22	2	9	5
1988	Ken Bouchard	24	0	0	0
1989	Dick Trickle	28	0	6	0
1990	Rob Moroso	25	0	0	0
1991	Bobby Hamilton	28	0	0	0
1992	Jimmy Hensley	22	0	0	0
1993	Jeff Gordon	30	0	7	1
1994	Jeff Burton	30	0	2	0
1995	Ricky Craven	31	0	0	0
1996	Johnny Benson	30	0	1	1
1997	Mike Skinner	31	0	0	2
1998	Kenny Irwin	32	0	1	1

MOST MULTIPLE WINSTON CUP CHAMPIONSHIPS

NUMBER	DRIVER	YEARS
7	Richard Petty	'64, '67, '71, '72, '74, '75, '79
	Dale Earnhardt	'80, '86, '87, '90, '91, '93, '94
3	Darrell Waltrip	'81, '82, '85
	Cale Yarborough	'76, '77, '78
	David Pearson	'66, '68, '69
	Lee Petty	'54, '58, '59
	Jeff Gordon	'95, '97, '98

ALL-TIME GRAND NATIONAL/WINSTON CUP SERIES RECORD HOLDERS (1949–1998)

Most wins in a career:	Richard Petty, 200
Most races in a career:	Richard Petty, 1,177
Most wins in a season:	Richard Petty, 27
Most consecutive wins:	Richard Petty, 10
Most wins from pole in a career:	Richard Petty, 61
Most wins from pole in a season:	Richard Petty, 5
Most wins at one racetrack:	Richard Petty, 15 (Martinsville and North Wilkesboro)
Most poles in a career:	Richard Petty, 127
Most poles in a season:	Bobby Isaac, 20
Most poles at one racetrack:	David Pearson, 14 (Charlotte Motor Speedway)
Best winning percentage in a career:	Tim Flock, 21.2
Best winning percentage in a season:	David Pearson, 61.1

Index

Photography Credits